REFUTATIONS

of the different sects of the pagans, of the religion of the Persians, of the religion of the sages of Greece, of the sect of Marcion

Eznik of Kolb,
Bishop of Bagrevand

Translated by: D.P. Curtin

REFUTATIONS

Copyright @ 2007 Dalcassian Publishing Company

All rights reserved. No part of this publication may be reproduced, distributed, or transmitted in any form or by any means, including photocopying, recording, or other electronic or mechanical methods, without the prior written permission of the publisher, except in the case of brief quotations embodied in critical reviews and certain other non-commercial uses permitted by copyright law. For permission request, write to Dalcassian Publishing Company at dalcassianpublishing at gmail.com

ISBN: 979-8-8690-9116-1 (Paperback)

Library of Congress Control Number:
Author: Curtin, D.P. (1985-)

Printed by Ingram Content Group, 1 Ingram Blvd, La Vergne, Tennessee

First printing edition 2007.

REFUTATIONS

REFUTATIONS

BOOK ONE
REFUTATION OF THE SECTS OF THE PAGANS

1. When man comes to discourse on the invisible (being) and his eternal power, because (man) is a corporeal (creature), he must clarify his intelligence, purify his thoughts, moderate the agitation of his movements, in order to be able to achieve the goal he has set for himself: for he who wants to look at the rays of the sun must remove from his eyes all trouble, all filth, all chastisement, so that these (causes of) obscurities, which would form ray around his eyelids, do not prevent him from contemplating the purity of the light.

Now, as the one and only essence is unexaminable, inaccessible by nature, before it's unexaminable nature we must make an offering of ignorance, and before its essence we must make a profession of knowledge and not of ignorance: for he who is must be eternal and without beginning; he has not received the beginning of being from anyone, he has no one above him whose cause we should esteem, or from whom we should think that he had the beginning of existence; for there is no one before him, no one after him is like him; for him there is no companion at his level, no essence contrary to him, no existence opposed to him, no material nature for his use, with which he does what he must do. But he is himself the cause of everything that has come to be and to exist, what is not and what is, such as the upper heavens and those in the heavens, the apparent heavens which are (composed) of waters, and the earth and all that is of it and in it; from him emanates everything, and he (emanates) from no one. He has, according to each class, given the beginning of being to invisible, incorporeal creatures, and to visible and corporeal creatures. As he is capable of giving vitality, so also, he is capable of bringing about the knowledge of his uncreated essence and of proceeding with the establishment of his creatures, according to their natures. He is admirable, not only because he brought into existence from nothing what did not exist, and from nothing he changed into something that which was not, but also because he preserved intact, inviolable his creatures, to whom he first gave without jealousy vitality, to manifest the magnificence of his goodness.

It is not that he would lack something, if for that he spared, by appropriating it alone, vitality; he would not be weak and without strength, if (even) he only thought of the strength of his person; nor devoid of knowledge, if he only kept knowledge for himself; nor devoid of wisdom, if, when he distributes his wisdom to others, some thought of reserve (for himself) should enter into the minds. But it is full of life and a source of vitality: it gives vitality to everything, and it itself remains full of incessant vitality. He strengthens the weak with great and mighty strength, and he himself does not lack strengthening power. He grants knowledge to all the ignorant, and he himself has all knowledge in abundance. He spreads inexhaustible wisdom to all, and he himself remains unshakably endowed with universal wisdom.

If the ever-gushing springs which have been established by his order, flow incessantly and do not dry up, if with their continuous jet they fill the needs of others, and themselves remain in the same continual abundance, how much more (rich) still is he who formed the abundance of their flow, he who is the source of goodness, he who made beautiful everything he made, that is to say, rational and irrational, intelligent and unintelligent beings, speaking and non-speaking, etc. ! To reasonable and intelligent beings, among the qualities particular to each, he assigned that of acquiring goodness, and not beauty; for he is the giver of beauty. As for goodness, he made man's free will the cause (of this virtue).

2. If then, those of the creatures which are beautiful are reputed to be produced by the good Creator, according to some, like the pagan Greeks, the Magi and the heretics, who admit an evil essence contrary to the good, (bad essence) that They call ὑλη, which translates: matter. Our first and sudden response is that, through the infinitely good Creator, nothing bad is done. There is nothing bad that is bad by nature; God is not the creator of bad things, but of good things.

Now, which of the creatures do they consider good, or which of them do they consider bad? because often the one they consider good, taken in isolation, without mixing with its companion, becomes harmful, which is attested by everyone in general. The sun is good, but without the mixture of air it burns and dries up; in the same way also the humid nature of the moon, without the mixture of the heat of the sun, is harmful, corrupting; and the air, without the humidity of dew, and without heat, is harmful, corrupting; and the waters water the soil of the earth and corrupt it; and the earth without waters is torn and split. Thus, the four natures (elements) from which results the composition, the constitution of this world, taken in particular, are corruptive of each other: mixed with their companion, they become useful and profitable. This is clearly the case for all those who want to learn.

There is therefore some hidden power which, from natures destructive to each other, through mixtures has made natures useful to each other. Those who have a right mind should not glorify the motive, but the mover. It is not those who walk, but rather the one who makes them walk that we must admire; for these (the moving objects), each by its changes, clearly show that there is a being which changes them thus: the sun, by its rising, its ascension, its setting, and the moon by its growth, its fullness , its decrease; and the rest of the creatures, each, according to their natures, by their movement and their rest. Now, it is not a healthy mind to leave aside the motor, the modifier, to worship mobile and modifiable objects and offer them adoration; because being moved and modified is not essential being; but either it is the product of someone, of something, or it is a being drawn from nothing. He who is and moves everything is himself neither moved nor changed; because it is essential and it is immobile.

3. He is an eternal essence, cause of the being of all; this is what those very people who introduced the cult of polytheism testify to; they argue thus: We, they say, as we are not capable of approaching the cause of everything, of the infinite, eternal, inaccessible being, for that, through (the intermediary of) other more humble beings , we worship him, and those (through whom) we worship him must also be honored with sacrifices and offerings.

If, as they testify, there is a single cause of everything, the essential and eternal being, it is obvious that other beings are not essential and eternal; and how will non-essential, non-eternal beings, with essential being, with eternal being, receive adoration? Especially corporeal and apparent beings, like your sun and your moon, and the stars, and the fire, and the water, and the earth which by the wise men and the pagans are honored.

But if any of these people say: It is good; it is an essence cause of everything, you say: now, if there is an essence which arouses, inspires everything in everything, if nothing is opposed to it, how can these ministers so good, so beneficent, who were established by it (essence), how do you order us to despise them?

We will say: These ministers so good, so beneficent, who were instituted by her (essence), we do not order to despise them, but we order iteratively not to offer to creatures the worship of the Creator; for there is no one who is beneficent or generous except he who has done everything without parsimony. He keeps rational, invisible beings alive and is not jealous; I say angels, the souls of men, inanimate objects, each in their place. Now, the sun is good and beautiful by nature, for us, for all the creatures under the heavens; it is useful for conservation, like a torch in a large house, lit between the roof and the ground, to dissipate, remove the darkness and gloom from the two large vases (or upper and lower cavities): but, for him (sun), if it is, if it is not, he knows nothing about it; for he is not among the number of reasonable and intelligent beings; likewise also with other inanimate creatures; and whether water, or fire, or earth, or air, whether they are, or whether they are not, they do not know. But the service for which they were instituted, they continually fulfill, under the direction of the one who formed them; and we do not despise these creatures, but also we do not worship them; but, in contemplating them, we glorify their author, their creator, because they are made for our needs and for the glory of their organizer.

How should we worship the sun, which is sometimes called as a servant to come and do the service for which it was destined, and sometimes flees as if in terror and gives way to darkness to fill the space in the great house (of this world), and from time to time turns to obscurity for the condemnation and shame of his worshippers; manifesting (and thus saying): I am not worthy of adoration, but he (is worthy of it), who keeps me and all the bright day, he who makes the dawn break; sometimes it obscures the sun, and it, being inanimate, seems to cry out with a sonorous voice: I am not worthy of receiving adoration, but of provoking adoration (for God); or (how to worship) the moon which every month withers and almost dies, then begins life again, in order to paint for you the example of the resurrection; or (how to worship) the air, which sometimes roars furiously at command, and sometimes ceases to roar, by the effect of a reprimand? Or (how to worship) the fire, whose author made you as the second creator; for, when you wish, you will set it on fire, and when you wish, you will prevent it from burning; or (how to worship) the earth, which we continually dig, which we continually tread, and into which we pour our refuse, the refuse of our animals; or (how to worship) the waters, which we continually drink, whose sweetness we change into putridity in our stomach, with which we purify our interior and exterior defilement?

From all this it is evident that what they hold to be gods, many neither respect nor honor. Moreover, a certain tremor, passion, seizes creatures when we give them the honor due to the Creator: the earth manifests this agitation by shaking, the stars by becoming dark, the air by becoming irritated, raging, the sea by the violence of its threatening waves; for, if the severity of the Creator did not restrain them, each of these creatures could, by itself, exterminate all (the reckless), in order to take revenge for their contempt for the Creator; the sea, hiding them in its depths, which, locked in a weak enclosure, cannot cross it, according to the order (of the master); the earth, by swallowing them up, which remains seated on nothing; but it does not suit him to return and make his inhabitants return to nothingness; or the wind, by the ruin of the impious, he who is the vitality of all beings having breath, and cannot stop this vitality without the order of the guardian of life; or the air, sometimes blowing icy cold, sometimes bringing excessive heat; and everything that is something would become nothing.

But now, like a chariot drawn by four horses, we see this world dragged by heat, by cold, by drought, and by humidity. A hidden power is the driver who maintains and subjects these four mutinous steeds to a peaceful and uniform pace. All the chariots are harnessed by beasts of the same race, but he (the chariot of the world) is the only one that is not harnessed by homogeneous beasts. The chariots which are harnessed by beasts of the same breed sometimes overturn, sometimes the steeds throw their driver into trouble and stop themselves. Sometimes they also cause the destruction of the tank. Even when the chariot is safe, the driver too, and the well-trained steeds, they only tend to rush straight ahead of them. But this marvellous chariot, harnessed by contrary and dissimilar beasts, driven by a hidden hand, does not only rush on one side straight ahead, but it carries itself on all sides, rushes everywhere, flies to all points, and is enough for everything. When he walks towards the east, there is nothing that prevents him from heading towards the west; and, when it goes towards the north, there is nothing that prevents it from flying towards the south; because the driver's hand is enough to make it arrive from all sides, and to launch it to the four corners of the universe.

4. Then, to these true assertions, they oppose inappropriate questions. Where do such contradictions come from, they say? For if God is the creator of good things and not of bad things, where does darkness come from? where do the evils come from, where do the sorrows come from, where do the anxieties come from, sometimes caused by the cold, sometimes by excessive heat? or where do the barbarities come from? for we see two men, of the same race, animated against each other; they crave each other's death and blood. Others search the tombs, and of the bodies that they have dug up and stripped, making an object of mockery, they show them in the light of the sun, and, this glorified corpse, so as not to take the trouble to hide it, they maybe throw it to the dogs. It sometimes happens that someone fleeing will go here and there to save his life;

let the other, inflamed with anger, running after him with the sword, not stop until he satisfies his fury. Where does this insatiable fury come from? The latter tears off the clothes of his companion, and, if he returns to the charge, he throws him out of the sun (of life); the one, having resolved to steal the rights of marriage of another, rushes illegally to a foreign land, and does not leave the right to be a father to the one who is married by law. Often battles take place where the guilty and the righteous are exterminated together, hence premature deaths, terrible illnesses. But what need do we have to list them one after the other? It is enough to say briefly where all this comes from, what is the principle, the maker of these disorders, if there is some evil power which allows all these disorders to occur, and which is itself the author; because to say that God is the creator of such things is inappropriate; evils do not derive their existence from him: how is it possible to believe them to be produced by God? for God is beneficent and creator of what is good, nothing that is evil comes near him; he does not delight in evil, he flees its actions and its creators. For evils are antipathetic to (God's) nature.

This is why they think that there was with him (God) something called ὑλη, that is, matter, from which he made all creatures, which he separated with an art and admirable wisdom, and adorned with amenities. From this matter we must believe the evils emerged, it (matter) which was ineffective and formless, and in confusion, winding here and there, came and went, and needed the skilful implementation of God. God did not let it (this matter) continually move in confusion, but he came to make the creatures, and from the grossness (of the matter) he wanted to extract good, excellent objects; he made, he took from matter, as much as he pleased to make creatures; everything that was filthy, muddy, unfit for creation, he left, and from this dregs come the evils of humanity.

5. Response. — Truly the evils that are happening put many people into perplexity, many wise men have done very great research on this subject. Some wanted to admit something without beginning with God; others, like him, a certain matter which they call ὑλη, saying that from it he made the creatures. Some have given up all research, because there is no end to these researches. But as for us, we had to, out of love for our friends, and not to confront our adversaries, because of our powerlessness, by taking refuge in the graces of God,

REFUTATIONS

(we had to) immerse ourselves in the search for discussions; especially because, full of hope, we are confident in the good and impartial dispositions of the listeners; hence it will be for them (the benefit) of learning the truth, and for us (the benefit) of not spending our speeches in vain; for it is not through injustice that we seek to overcome, but through righteousness we seek to learn the truth.

From this it is evident that two uncreated things cannot be together; for where two beings are together, there must be something which separates them. Now, how do they view God? as being in some place, in all ὕλη, or in a single part of ὕλη? If they say that all God is in all ὕλη, however great they call God, ὕλη finds himself greater than God; for the one in which someone is, the one in whom he is, is found greater than the one who is in him, since he was able to contain him entirely. If they say that God is in some part only of ὕλη, then ὕλη is found to be a thousand times greater than God, since a part of ὕλη was capable of containing all of God; and, if God is neither in ὕλη, nor in any part of ὕλη, it is evident that there was some other medium between them two, greater than them both; and not only two beings are found without beginning, but even three beings. God, ὕλη, and especially this environment greater than the two (other beings).

Now, if he was once a ὕλη without ornament, without actuality, without form, and God adorned him; because, from this bad state, he wanted to make it pass to a better state; therefore, there was a time when God was in things without ornament, without actuality, without form, and it was necessary that, like ὕλη, God himself was agitated in confusion.

If in everything in ὕλη, as they say, was God, when he brought (ὕλη) to ornament, to actuality, to form, he himself (God) in whom could he collect himself? because it was not possible for him to meditate anywhere. Did he himself (God), with ὕλη, also bring himself to the state of ornament, of actuality, of form; because there was nowhere to gather? which is the ultimate impiety.

REFUTATIONS

But if they say that ὕλη was in God, after that it should be inquired how (was there) separation from him, like the brutes in the middle of the air, which are in the air and separated from the air, or (was it) in a (fixed) place like the waters in the earth?

Ὕλη, they say, was improper, without ornament, without topicality, bad; if, according to their thoughts, it is so, then the place of evils was God; for monstrous things, without ornament, were in him; which is an incredible injustice, to think that God was once the receptacle of evils, then the creator of evils! Moreover, he was inseparable even if he was there as if in a fixed place.

6. Now we must come to the causes of evils, and show where evils come from, that God is not the cause of evils, by the very fact that they place ὕλη near him. Now, what ὕλη do they place in the hands of God? Is it not the ὕλη from which he drew, made the world? which was without form, without ornament, without actuality; because we see this world (coming) to different forms, to ornaments, to actualities; therefore, of forms, of ornaments, of actualities, the creator is God, and (he is not) of natures. But, if it is the work of the Creator to make natures, and not only ornaments, actualities and forms, it is obvious that it is superfluous to think that of any matter present with him, God made this world, but (he made it) from nothing and from what did not exist. What's more, we see men who, from what does not exist, make something; so, your builders, not (with) cities make cities, nor (with) temples temples. As they absolutely cannot do anything, the stones they arrange into buildings are no longer called stones, but cities or temples; because this city, this temple, is the work, not of nature, but of art which, (it, is) in nature; and art does not receive the knowledge of art from any object present there, which is in nature, but (it receives it) from the accidents which happen in natures themselves. Because it is not in the personal state, coming from (beings) personal, that it is possible to show art, but (product) of accidents which happen. As the blacksmith does forging, the carpenter does carpentry; because man exists prior to art; but art does not exist if man does not exist first. Hence it must be said that art is in no way appropriate for men. If this is the case for men, how much more appropriate is it to think of God, that not only of actualities, of ornaments, of forms, he is the creator, but that of nothing he is capable of making the natures, and not that it is an actual matter, from which God (has drawn and) extracts

the good in one heap, and the muddy evil in another heap, from which that which is muddy strives to disturb which is clear.

7. The evils that happen, where do they come from?

We will also ask: Are the evils that occur people or products of people?

They say: It is appropriate to think that (evils) are produced by people.

And ὕλη, which they say is unproductive, is unformed; how unproductive, shapeless could he give birth to products in others, if it is not that evils come from accidents, and not from him; for murder is not a person, and fornication is not a person, nor are the other evils one after the other. But, as science is called the scientist, art the artist, medicine the doctor, not that they are persons, but of things from which we take the names, so also the evils of accidents take their name.

If they imagine another instigator, promoter who casts evils into the minds of men, and the act he does takes the name of wickedness. But you have to know that what someone does is not that someone themselves; just as the potter, when he makes vases, is not himself a vase; but he is a maker of vases, from which he takes the name of his profession; Likewise also the evildoer, from the action of doing evil, takes the name of wickedness, whether he is a fornicator or a murderer. Therefore, with reason, men are said to be the authors of evils; for they are themselves the causes of doing and not doing; and evils we must not call people, but products of people, and bad (products). If they remain in this stupidity, (thinking) that precisely without actuality, without form was ὕλη, and that God brought it to ornament, to forms, to products, then they suppose God causes evils. It would be better for such an object to have remained formless, unproductive, than to arrive at products, forms, and become the cause of the ills of others; for what could an individual be if he were formless? There is more, to say formless, obviously shows (that it is a question of) objects having form. Now, if there was something with personality, form, it is superfluous to say its creator, God.

REFUTATIONS

But by this very fact, they say, that from non-actuality, and from the monster-state (God) made pass (this thing) to the state of ornament, of form, with reason he is called creator.

This looks like this. When, (with) stones someone makes constructions, of appropriation, of the arrangement only he is creative, and not of nature itself. Now, for what purpose did God make formlessness, for a better state or for a worse state? If they say for a better state, then, as for the evils that come, they must seek where they come from? Therefore, these products have not remained as they were, but, because they have been converted to a better state, only better they will appear; but, if they have turned to a worse state, they (the pagans) can say that God is the cause of the evils, since he himself had converted these products to a better state.

But they say that God separated (that which was) clear into one side, from which he made the creatures, and left (that which was) mire.

We will say: Since God could clarify this (impure mixture), even eliminate the evils, and he did not want to eliminate them, therefore it must be said to be the cause of the evils; for from one half (of the matter) he made the good creatures, and left the other half as it was to become (a means of) corruption for the good creatures. If anyone examines things truthfully, he finds ὕλη fallen into a danger more immense than (that of) the first confusion; for, before the sorting and awareness of the dangers of evils, ὕλη was in tranquillity and carelessness, and now, as a result of the acquired perception of evils, he finds himself in trouble and perplexity. If you want, take an example from the man himself; for, before taking form and becoming alive, (man) was a non-participant in evils, and, when he comes to the state of man, then he is inclined to evils by his own free will; in the same way also, (as a result) of goodness, what they say emanates from God, ὕλη, finds itself arrived at a worse state.

But, if God, through his inability to remove evils, has left them as they are; by this very fact, they impute impotence to God, whether he is impotent by nature, or whether, through fear, he was defeated by another being stronger

REFUTATIONS

than himself: if they say (God) prey to apprehension, overcome by a being greater than themselves, they must admit the evils that are tyrannical judges of the will of God; and why, according to their reasoning, should not evils be gods, they who can overcome God?

8. Then again we will ask, concerning ὕλη: Is it a simple nature or (formed) by aggregation; for the different accounts of things lead us to such an examination; for, if simple nature were ὕλη and of a single form, (as) this world is established, composed of aggregations, of different natures and mixtures, it is impossible to say that it is material; because it is not possible for aggregations to have, (to draw) their constitution from a simple nature, because aggregations are added, (are formed) from simple (united) natures.

If simple natures (ὕλη) were joined (composed), there was therefore a time when ὕλη was not there, since, by the addition of simple natures, ὕλη was: from which (it follows that) ὕλη appears created and not uncreated; for, if by aggregation was ὕλη, (as) aggregations draw their personality from simple natures, there was then a time when there was not even ὕλη, before there arose simple (natures) between them, and, s 'there was not a time when ὕλη was not, therefore there was not a time when ὕλη was not uncreated; for, if God were still and simple natures also uncreated, from which ὕλη (came out aggregated), it is evident that there were not only two uncreated beings, but five.

And now let us see, were these natures in harmony with each other, from which ὕλη (came out) aggregated, or were they contrary to each other? Now, here we see these natures contrary to each other; for water is opposed to fire, darkness to light, heat to cold, moisture to dryness. Contrary and harmful to oneself is not (each of these natures), but to its companion. From this it is evident that (these natures) are not (born) from a single matter, and that a single matter does not come from four contrary (natures); thus, when matter came into existence, it was not to itself that it was opposed, but to its companion, like white to black, sweet to bitter.

REFUTATIONS

9. Now therefore, leaving the question ὕλη, which they call matter of all, let us come to the question of evils, which they consider to emanate from ὕλη; for, when evils are evidently demonstrated not to be in the state of persons, hence ὕλη is also convinced to have never been, nor nature in the state of person.

Now, concerning the evils of humanity, we will ask: Are these evils produced by people, or are they people? for all the movements which take place in the body and in the mind cannot be said to be man, but voluntary movements; for man is in the state of a person, and evils are not in the state of persons, such as murder and fornication, which are the fact of his morals.

Now, if these acts are creatures in the state of persons, we must also, as to the cause they admit, consider them creatures in the state of persons; for he, of whom a part is a creature, it is evident that he is entirely a creature, and he, of whom a part is not a creature, it is evident that he himself is not a creature at all: therefore he was a time when there was no complete creator, before God had made man, from which evils come; because, of the part of evils man finds himself creator; From there, it is obvious that even evils are the proper creator of God: let it never happen that God is the cause of evils! but (the cause) is he who, by his own will, will commit the act of these evils; and to him by whom evil is done, the name of wickedness is precisely applied, as we have previously said.

10. Now let us come to the actual examination of things, so that when precisely the assaults take place, they will easily deploy the manifestation of their arguments.

Now, will they say God is good and beneficent? They must call him good and beneficent, that no wickedness should come near him; and if this is so, first with regard to fornication and lust, we will ask, then with regard to other such (excesses): If by the order of God these evils were committed, why Are the creators of these evils (God) taking revenge? but by the very fact that according to these wicked acts he takes revenge, it is evident that he does not accept evils, but that he hates them and that he launches rigorous punishments on their

REFUTATIONS

authors, by whom, according to their stupidity, the admonitions of God are esteemed scourges. As even now murderers, when they come to punishment, do not call those who inflict these punishments on them beneficent, but evil; for such is the manner of evildoers: what is justice they call injustice. So that we do not say anything of the sort, let us consider evils not as personal, but as products of the will.

Lust and fornication happen through the intimate approach of man and woman. If a lawfully married man has commerce with his wife for filiation and generation, good is that commerce; but if a man, leaving his own wife, steals the marriage of another, he is committing an act of wickedness; and, although the commerce is the same, the example of this commerce is not the same; for one is the lawful father of children, and the other a thief (of paternity). Same reasoning also on the subject of lust; if, for filiation, a man approaches his wife, it is right; but if, out of lust, he covets (and seeks) carnal pleasures elsewhere, this is a great iniquity. It is obvious that things become bad, even though the need (and use) is not enshrined in the laws.

Concerning the murder, still same speech. When someone kills a man caught in adultery, causing the fatal blow to fall on him because of his audacity, he does no harm; but, if someone kills an innocent man, who has done nothing reprehensible to him, (if he kills him) either to steal his property, or to divide his property, he commits wickedness. The act is the same on both sides, but the example is not the same.

As for taking something, same reasoning. He who takes from a master some present or some gift from a friend, does nothing wrong; but he who violently takes something from a poor person is committing an act of wickedness. The action of taking of these two men is the same, but the example is not the same.

Likewise also, for divine worship, by example evil is demonstrated. If it is the true God that a man honors, he does an excellent action; but if, having left the true (God), to stones and woods as (if it were) God, he offers worship, he does incredible harm; for he has turned the example of his duties into unseemly things. If a man makes an image, not for the love of a friend who, through (the effect of) death, has disappeared from his sight, or to show off his talent; but (if), taking (this image) as an object of worship, he worships it as God, (this man) acts of wickedness.

Thus, in the disposition of certain things, the intention of the worker does evil; like iron, sometimes for good is used, and sometimes for evil; for if a man makes it stake, scythe, pruning hook, for good things the iron has been used; but if a man does it with sword, spear, javelin or other weapon, which is harmful to humanity, (this man) does a work of wickedness. The cause of the evil is therefore the worker, and not the iron.

11. Now, say (the pagans), will men have these movements of themselves, or do (these movements) come to them from God? or would there be some other (being) who provoked them in men?

That these effects emanate in men from God does not seem appropriate to say. But having free will was the property of the first man created by God, and from him (first man) his successors inherited it. Now, man, having received free will, submits to whomever he wishes; which is a great favor granted to man by God; for every other (creature) is necessarily subject to divine orders. If you speak of the heavens, they remain fixed and do not move from their assigned place; if you want to talk about the sun, it accomplishes the movement imprinted on it, and cannot deviate from its course; but necessarily he obeys the order of his lord; similarly, also we see the earth solidified. It carries (within itself) the order of the master, and all other beings of the same kind are subject to the orders of the Creator and cannot do anything other than what they were intended for. Therefore, we praise them for thus observing the orders (which they received).

But man, having received free will, subjects himself to whomever he wishes. He is neither constrained by the necessity of nature, nor stopped by that power which has been given to him for good; but by his obedience only he finds advantage and profit, and by disobedience harm; and this, we say, not for the misfortune of man, but for his greater good; for if he were like an individual of other natures, who necessarily serve God, he would not be worthy of receiving the reward due to his voluntary action, but he would be like an instrument of the Creator. Although the Creator pushed him to evil or good, neither blame would be (due) to him nor praise; but the cause would be the one who pushed it. Moreover, man from then on would know nothing better; for he would not be capable of anything other than what he would have been appropriate for. But God wanted to honor man in this way, that in order for him to become knowledgeable about good, he gave him free will, with the help of which man can do what he will, and (God) warns us to turn this free will to good.

Like a father, when he urges his son, so that he can learn some science, not to slack off from his studies, he urges him to progress in good, because he knows that (his son) can do progress, it requires application to the study for which it was intended; in the same way we must also think of God, that he disposes man to listen to his orders. But as to the power to do what he pleases, God does not take away that power, by which man can obey or disobey the commands of God. But it engages and disposes man to desire what is good, so that he may become worthy of the great benefits (of God) if he obeys God; but in such a way that he has the power not to obey; for it was not inconsiderately that God wanted to grant man this present, which is eternal indestructibility. Now, it would be inconsiderate to give such a gift to one who did not have the power of both acts, (knowing) to obey what God would want, and not to obey what (God) would not approve. ; but this is just, when a man receives the worthy reward for what he has done.

How would the choice of actions appear if man did not have the power of both sides: to obey and not to obey? It is therefore evident that man was created free to do good or to commit evil; not that there was any evil before him to which he had to bear himself, but there was only before him the choice: to obey God or to disobey him, a fact which man understood to be only the cause of the evil; for the first man created received an order from God, and, not having obeyed this divine order, he turned to evil; hence came the beginning of the evils.

Hence (it follows that) no one can show evil to be uncreated and personal; from the Creator it does not emanate, but it arrived by the audacity of the rebellious man and provoked by the doctrine of someone; for such was not how man was naturally constituted: no one can prove that. If man had received (as a share) such a nature; therefore, according to his created nature, the doctrine of the divine books would not have been offered to him; as divine language says somewhere, * from childhood, man has devoted himself to the cares of evil, to show that, he who devotes himself (to evil), indulges in it voluntarily and not by (force).), by someone's tyranny.

Therefore, impudence alone which is committed outside the will of God must be considered the cause of evils. There must be no other hidden doctor, instigator, tyrant, who wanted to strip man of his perfections. If then they wish to further examine the cause, let them consider the desire which came to man as the (true) cause; and if, touching on this desire, they carefully examine where it came from, we will say that it came from the additional honor given to man; for man alone was made according to the image and likeness of God. Now, if by this they mean God causes evils, they fall outside of (all) judicious thought. If God had taken something from himself and given it to man, perhaps precisely as the cause of evils, would he be regarded as the donor? but if, as he was, God preserved himself, if he wanted to make man like this, the cause of evils is the envious person; for, when a man has ten slaves, and he retains one in slavery, registers the other as adopted son, if the one rushes on this one and kills him; is it that, as the cause of evil, we must look at the master, he who took nothing from one of his slaves, but gave to the other (slave)?

12. But they still ask this: If there was no evil present, whence (come) the serpent, whom you call Satan, foresaw the circumstances of evil?

We say that Satan, in his wickedness, foresaw man's revolt against God; for this very reason, he disposed man; as, when someone has an enemy (who), hiding his enmity, secretly wants to harm him; although he does not know the (means) and circumstances to be able to do harm, he turns, he interferes in seeking (all) the means; then, having found the (propitious) time, when one of his enemy's doctors order him not to touch such and such a thing, not to taste such and such food, in order to thus be able to achieve health, that one (the perfidious) having heard (the prescription), with the feigned appearance of friendship, will blame the doctor, will, through his insinuations, regard his salutary prescriptions as harmful, will give prescriptions contrary to those of the doctor, and thereby will harm the sick. It is not that, previously, (this enemy) knew the circumstances (or means) to be able to do harm; but, according to the doctor's prescription, having found these means, it became harmful; in the same way we also think with regard to Satan, that he was jealous of the first man created, but that he did not know the circumstances (or means) to be able to do harm; for there was nothing evil there present, from which he could take (draw knowledge of these) circumstances. Instructed according to the command of God which was given to man, to prevent him from eating (the fruit) of a deadly plant, (Satan) proposed to man (his perfidious advice). It is not that this plant was useless for human nutrition, nor harmful by its nature, and that for this reason man was prevented from tasting it; but disobedience (of the man) was the cause of his death, as (happens) to the prevaricator who transgresses the order of the master which will have been imposed on him.

Now, the enemy of man led him to transgress the command of God, not that he knew perfectly well whether by doing so he could do any harm to man; but he remained uncertain whether it would or would not be (thus). Then, after the judgment of God which came against man, because of his transgression, (Satan) understood that the orders of God caused his death, and that, precisely, they were punished, he and the man whom he it had led to rebellion, to tasting (the fruit) of the tree which, not deadly by nature, but according to the threats of God, became the cause of these events.

As we cannot indict a doctor for having predicted in advance how a man will be able to return to health (if) he (the sick person), leaving aside the doctor's prescriptions, listens to the enemy who will give advice harmful; thus, the cause of the damage should not be believed to be the fact of the doctor who previously announced (the opposite), but the fact of the enemy who, according to the doctor's prescription, found (the means of) harm; Likewise also of Satan we say: being an enemy of men, he did not know the circumstances of evils; but, advised according to the command of God, he wanted to harm man so that (man) if, without the will of God, tasted of the fruit of the tree, would receive death as punishment; for if God had not previously warned man not to eat food from this tree, and the man had not knowingly eaten it, there would have been no penalty of death for him; or, as if, without knowing it, he had eaten it, or again, for not abstaining from the fruit of the tree, he would not have been liable to punishment; for the child who, hitherto nourished on milk, throws himself on some other food, must not be punished, but prevented, seeing that, by the absence of milk, he has carried himself to this act. Moreover, the serpent, who is Satan, was justly punished because of his implacable enmity for man.

Therefore, the beginning of evils is jealousy, we say, jealousy conceived especially because of the great honors granted to man, and evils come from his disobedience; for God thus honored man magnificently, and (man) rebelling, rejected the commands of God; from which (it follows that) all the evil that happens is not evil by nature, we know that, but, because without the will of God certain things are done, they become evil.

Furthermore, since Satan came from God, he knew that if anyone does not obey God, it is evil, not good; for he would have been a creature deprived of sense by God, if he had not known that what is done according to the will of God is good, and that what happens outside of his will is evil; and, for this, God torments (Satan) precisely, because (Satan) knows good and does not do it. He is taught about evil and does not flee it. God has not constituted him evil, nor evil-doing, nor tempter, even though, by his means, he purifies the righteous tested (by temptation). (Satan) therefore did not find himself evil, nor being uncreated and opposed to God; but, intelligently done by God, provided (with the means) to know that it is wrong to resist the command of God; and his action of going to what he knew to be evil, we call revolt, impudence, not that this impudence is in the state of a person and as a being previously found, come to the knowledge of Satan; but it was as something resulting from the accidents of his will.

Moreover, concerning man, we say precisely, he suffers the fatal judgment for what he does; for he will voluntarily seek the teaching of things from which, when he wishes, he can abstain; for he has the power to will and not to will that after which he runs, as well as the power to do what he wills.

REFUTATIONS

13. Since, they say, you do not mean God the creator of evils, but (you want them to emanate) from men, at the instigation of Satan, (by his influence) on them, who obey him and that 'he deceived, then men suffer a just punishment; because they could cut off, cast away evils from them, and they did not want to. Now, regarding Satan itself, we will ask: Did God make him as he is? if he were not such (as he is), did God dispose him to do evil?

If such (as he is) had God made him, he should not draw punishment (from Satan), because (Satan) has preserved the condition of nature in which God made him. Whoever, not through the effect of his will, commits any act, must not suffer punishment for this act. But whoever voluntarily can act, and commits an act of perversity, is precisely punished, because he did not stop at what God wants. If then (Satan) was made good by God, and he of himself turned his will to evil, away from good, it is with justice that punishment is taken (from Satan) for the acts that 'he dared to commit; for Satan, we know, was not made Satan by God; but this name of Satan he received as his own name, because of his error; for Satan, according to the language of the Hebrews and Syrians, is translated as: lost; but a certain force for good has been constituted in him by God; and Satan, animated by hatred against man, voluntarily became his tempter. Having left due submission to God, he began to disobey Him, to teach men to resist God's commands; and, like a rebel, (Satan) kept himself far from God; (this is what) the divine language testifies, which calls him dragon (saying that:) * by order, he killed the rebellious dragon. Right is this word. God killed the dragon, thereby giving him power to trample it under foot. Revolted, as the Scripture calls it. If as he was made by God he had remained, (Scripture) would not call him rebellious; because whoever rebels leaves aside his commitment, by which he shows that he is not uncreated; for if he were uncreated, he would change nothing in his nature of being; for it is impossible for a person's nature, without his will, to be sometimes good, sometimes evil.

14. But if (Satan) was not uncreated, they say, according to your Satan, if such he was not made by God, then he of himself turned away from good to evil, that is to say, from obedience to disobedience; you said that. Did God know if (Satan) would become like this (rebellious), or did He not know? If (God) knew it and did (Satan); God himself is the cause of (Satan's) malversation. If

REFUTATIONS

God did not know, how did he create this being, not knowing what he would become?

To attribute ignorance to God is incredible madness, because only he has foreknowledge of the future. But, as beneficent essence is God, he did not want to hide his supreme greatness. This is why he knew in advance that Satan would go astray, and would cause men not to listen to his orders, and God, to allow man's free will to manifest itself, made Satan, so that the superabundance of his goodness became evident to men, because of the forgiveness made to men of their previously committed sins; for, when they see Satan falling into impiety, and not exterminated, even regarding their sins, they will understand that it is a means of forgiveness through penitence, so that the goodness of God may be manifested, and that men recognize his grace; for, if it had not been so, we would not have been informed of the goodness of God.

God, they say, after Satan had gone astray and deceived men, why did he not exterminate him, to prevent him from destroying a multitude (of victims)?

It is not that God was not powerful enough to exterminate Satan; for there is no impotence at all in God; but it would not have been a big deal for God to kill Satan himself, and to make one of his tiny creatures return to nothingness; (God did not want) people to think that, in order not to endure the wickedness of Satan, he had killed him. Secondly, it is that the goodness of God would have remained unknown to men to come if he had killed Satan in advance; for no one would have had (then) a (certain) sign to call God beneficent; but perhaps the thought had entered (into the minds of men) that Satan was a being equal to God, and that God (for this reason) had hastened to exterminate him. Therefore, God preserved him and did not destroy him, so that men, when they are taught what is good, will be able to overcome Satan, unlike those who were first overcome by Satan.

What is even greater, more astonishing, is that the man of God, armed with the help of God, after having fought, will defeat Satan. Like a master of arms, by all possible means and blows having endeavored to instruct his students, to show all the accidents and circumstances of the fights, so that they can defeat their adversaries, will send (his students) to fence against these adversaries, warning them to pay close attention to victory, even to the point of despising life; for it is better that for (the glory of) their name they die, than to remain alive and be dishonored. These (the students), engraving in their minds the recommendation of the master, and the advantages of victory, will prevail over their adversaries, all crowned will arrive near the master; and, as a sign of their (happy) struggle against their said adversaries, their master will bring their crown. But, if (these students) have not engraved in their minds the lessons of the master of arms, they cannot aspire to victory and crowns; they are defeated, dishonored by their adversaries. Rightly from now on they are insulted, tormented, and even death for the penalty of their cowardice they have to suffer.

Likewise, we must understand, touching God, that by his commandments he guides men well, to crown the victor and make the coward (blush) with shame. If a man counts the commandments of God as nothing, when (that man) strives and fights against the tempter, he will be speedily defeated; for he does not have the sign of victory; and (it is) precisely (that he) suffered the punishment of such a blow, because he was not like his companion who fought and conquered.

So, for this, God has let Satan live (to serve) in the exercises of the struggles of the world, so that when the champions (of God) fight and defeat Satan, the glory of the first victory (of Satan) will be broken by these men of today, who, through the effect of their great desire for good, will have defeated (Satan), and the sign of victory, they will erect as a sign of their glorious exploits; because thrown, trampled under our feet, Satan defeated succumbs and dies; he is struck down by the effect of our passion for good, and delivered to (complete) defeat.

15. Now, after acquiescing to this, the fools, they put forward the same thing. Evils are by nature, they say, and not products of the will.

REFUTATIONS

We say: If by nature they are (evils), why are laws established by kings, rigors by princes, punishments by judges? Is it not to eradicate evils? Moreover, if evils are by nature, the legislator must not pass laws, nor the prince impose penalties on the wrongdoer. Why should we punish someone who, not by will, is wicked, whom we should take pity on, and not impose (severe) penalties on him?

Therefore, if this man debauches with a woman, he should not be charged; for (it was) not by will, as they say, (that he) was inclined to evil, but (he) was forced to it by nature. If his son, taking a sword, attacks him, let him not be charged; for, not by will, he walks; but evil leads him to this. If a man is insulted by a neighbor and a friend, let him not insult him in turn, but let him even have more pity on him; because (it is) not he (the neighbor, the friend) who insults him, but (it is) evil which tyrannically pushes (the insulter). Likewise, when a daughter despises her mother, a daughter-in-law her father-in-law, a wife her husband, a slave her master, and a brother her brother, let them not bring anything untoward in the minds of those who have been despised, but let them (on the contrary) have pity on these people, as (people) tyrannized by evil.

Now, if we see that the king takes revenge for his laws (violated) and by this revenge (justly taken) stops the damage, the judge more or less strongly chains the thief and the bandit to take away the means of harm; a father, condemning his perverse son to death, hands him over to the judges; all the others (men) take revenge for the insults (which they experience) either by themselves or by the princes; it is obvious that the evils that are committed are born of will and not natural; but come on, this man immersed in concupiscence bind him strongly and strike him roughly, see if there is still in him (the slightest) memory of his concupiscence; and truly, it is not in vain that these words of the wise were said:
* Let the slave who does not hear with his ear, let him hear with his back.

Moreover, on the other hand, we can understand that the nature of man is desirous of good and not of evil; for the fornicator who commits fornication, while he is still even in the act of fornication, if anyone calls him a fornicator, he becomes angry. The whore, who prostitutes herself publicly, does not like to hear the name prostitution. Likewise, the thief and the bandit, and even (other) criminals, although they commit crimes, do not want to accept the name of crimes. Moreover, the deceiver in a state of deceit who, through gentle (and insidious) schemes, wants to harm his companion, hides his deceit, and, as if he were giving some good advice, seducing him, he throws in the damage (of perdition) the innocent; but, if he does not put on this exterior of goodness and does not act sullen, he cannot turn away from equity the one who knows equity.

Moreover, when someone wants to bring a severe prince to gentleness, he cannot openly say to him: You are severe; but approaching him with sweet words, he implores him, (saying): Lord, you are gentle and beneficial to all, everyone considers you righteous, and so he can gently soften the severity of the prince, bend it and bring it to what is right and worthy. Likewise, with an irritated and saddened person, with an envious man, we approach gently and soothe him. And from this it is evident that the nature of men is desirous of good and not of evil.

If the ferocity of wild beasts makes (the pagans) think that it is evil by nature, let them know that half of the brutes were made for the needs (of man), like the herd and the small cattle, and everything good to eat and wear. (The other) half (of the brutes were made) to strike fear into the minds of men; for if wild beasts are terrible, dragons, serpents and other harmful animals, and man is so superb that, crossing the limits of the fear of God, he resists him, if these terrifying beasts do not were not, how much more (man) would never stand in duty!

What's more, the very things that are believed to be bad by fools often become useful and protect against death. What is eviller than the serpent, and from him (however comes) theriac. Thus, from murderous drugs, which were composed by the perfidy of men, the result was not death, but healing. If by nature an evil thing were the serpent, or the creature of some evil being, there would be absolutely nothing useful in it, and it would never lose its ferocity. We see it even by the art of enchanters becoming tamed; he is for them like a rope dancer, often he even lives in the same house without doing any harm to the inhabitants.

REFUTATIONS

Now, if it is a pagan who regards certain objects as evil by nature, he will be refuted by his fellow artists, the snake breeders. (These people), who know how to tame serpents so well, to the point of calling them by enchantments into houses, of offering them food, as (did) the Babylonians to the dragon they adored, but their beloved god killed it to make it his ordinary food.

If it is a magician who calls wild beasts bad creatures, because of their ferocity, he will be refuted, blamed by common sense; for, if wild beasts are creatures of evil and the earth a creature of good, how can (she), a creature of good, be the nurse mother of the creatures of evil, who are nourished by them and rest in her bosom? for two things contrary to each other are destructive of each other, as light (is destructive) of darkness, and heat of frost.

Therefore, if wild beasts were creatures of evil and the earth a creature of good, consuming them would be a duty for the earth, and not maintaining them; (it should) destroy them and not spread them. If then the earth nourishes the wild beasts and does not destroy them, it is evident that by the same creator, by whom the earth is produced, the wild beasts were made. And above all these ferocious beasts, which they say are produced by the bad creator, clearly show that they are not just earth, by the very fact that they are nourished by the earth, that they inhabit it, and, having wandered on the earth, they become earth again.

Moreover, if evil (creatures) were made by evil, nothing useful would be found (result) from them, but they would be entirely evil. Now, if we see that the skins of one part (of wild beasts) serve as a covering for our nudity, that the fat of some serves for lighting, that of others (is good) for the limbs, like fat of the lion, the bear and other animals successively; it is evident that by the creator of good (these creatures) were made, by the very fact that we find in them something useful; for a beast which is (creature) evil, everything in it is harmful, both the skin and the flesh. But we put on their skin, and it does us no harm, and even if someone were to take their flesh, even their heart, and eat it, it would not harm him, like a wild boar, which is the most fierce of all wild beasts, we eat the flesh and it does no harm; in the same way, if anyone eats their flesh (that of wild beasts), it will not harm him.

In the herds, which they say were made by the good creator, there is something harmful. Eating the flesh of a bull is nourishment for the body, but if one drinks blood (of a bull), he is lost. Likewise, also in plants, there are some which, taken in isolation, are deadly, and (which), mixed with other plants, become a remedy for various pains. Mandrake, if one eats even a little of it, is deadly, and, mixed with other roots, it is a soporific for people deprived of sleep. And millet, if someone eats it in very hot weather, as it is refreshing, it dissipates the great heat from the stomach, and if someone eats it in cool weather, it hurts. And the water extracted (from millet) unmixed, if anyone drinks it, he is a dead man. And the semen, diluted in water, if anyone drinks it, he removes it from concupiscence. And hemp is a shrub whose seed is a remedy which is still used to stop concupiscence. And hemlock which, taken alone in a fixed time, is deadly, (it is also) through it that doctors have imagined destroying inveterate fevers. And the titinaille is a species which alone is murderous; mixed with another drug, it is a remedy against bile and protects against death.

So, for not looking righteously (and attentively) at these inconsistent things, they imagined that there was something inherently evil. But God, with so much wisdom, made man (in such a way) that he could benefit even from these drugs; (that even in those) which are deemed harmful, he can still, by (certain) means, find utility, (as) in resuming the conduct of fools, (by proving to them) that there is nothing which is evil by nature.

16. But, although these people do not believe in divine laws, let us not deprive our friends of a direct answer.

So much evil did not exist by nature in wild beasts, before God, having brought these new creatures to the new created man, had enjoined him to impose names on them; and, if these creatures had not approached (man), how would he have assigned a name to each of them according to their species? Therefore, if these beasts approached and became familiar with man, it is evident that they were neither bad nor harmful to man. But after his transgression of God's orders, (to man) were given these terrifying beasts to stop the pride of this earthly being who was made of earth and had to return to earth.

REFUTATIONS

This first state of harmlessness of animals towards man (is a fact to which) their current taming, their familiarity, testify; for a (man) raises the cub of a wolf, and (the wolf), like the cubs of a dog, with familiarity attaches itself (to this man). Another (man) having raised the cub of a lion, he accustoms it to embraces and caresses, to the point of hugging his infant, and if someone approaches, (the animal), not forgetting the morals of his ferocity, melts on him; (the master), then scolding the animal like (he would scold) a dog, suppresses its indomitable ferocity. Another (man), having raised the cub of a bear, teaches him to dance, and, training him in the ways of men, destroys his fierce morals. Some other person, having caught wild monkeys, trains them to be pranksters, jokers, and all sorts of mischievous tricks. Others, having taken basilisks in feminine forms, by enchantments bring them into familiarity with man, thus destroying their murderous venom.

Now, if wild beasts were bad by nature, it would not be possible for these harmful beings, with their evil character, to adopt tame ways, and if, as for excessive heat and freezing cold, they believe them to be made to harm by the evil creator, let them therefore know: that, if the snow and the frost did not harden the mountains, the roots of the plants would not grow, and, if the great heat did not warm the plains, the fruits would not come.

17. If evils and diseases and premature deaths, and death itself, they think all these produced by some evil creator, if they believed in the divine laws, (arguing) from these laws themselves, we we would respond. But, since they suppose all these disorders to be produced by the bad creator, we will ask them: Of the creator of goods, and (of the creator) of evils, which is more powerful? If they say that the creator of goods is (the most) powerful, they are lying; for if he were more powerful than the creator of evils, he would not give him (permission) to cast his curses on good creatures, and, moreover, he should not give him any place in his territory; for if (the creator of good) were at all powerful, he would first separate his domain from (that of the creator of evil), and then, then, his creatures, whatever might (his enemy) do.

But they will say this: Could he, the good, ward off the (evil) of his good creatures, if he were not powerful? If they say that good was powerful, then let them know that if it could ward off evil, and did not ward it off, it itself is the cause of the damage; and, if he could not ward off evil, he found that more powerful than him was the evil which violently persecuted him, and corrupted his good creatures. Even more false is what they say: in the end, the victor over evil is good; for he who at first cannot conquer, it is evident that in the end he cannot conquer.

But many pains and death are the causes which we have to set forth in truthful terms. First this (knowing) that when man had transgressed the order of God he was then under (the blow) of pain and death; for (God) said to the woman: * With pain and sadness you will give birth; and (he said) to man: By the work and the sweat of your face you will eat your bread, until you return to the earth from which you were made; for you were slime and to slime you will return. From this it is evident that, although the nature of man, for (man is a) corporeal being, was known to be under the influence of pain and death, but, if (man) had remained (submitted) to his command, the author of his life would have kept him alive. He who from nothing was able to create the breath of man, and always keeps him alive and immortal, he could in the same way for his body that he created (and took) from the earth keep it alive.

18. But when they hear this, the enemies of the truth, with different weapons fight against the evidence; for half (of them) say that it was not possible for a corporeal being to remain immortal; and others say, for the very reason that the body did not last with breath to live a long time, it must die, not lasting.

But the former are refuted by (the example of) Elijah and Enoch who, until now, are alive; and the others are confounded by the general and universal resurrection; for if now, because the bodies are not durable, they die, then and in the resurrection, according to their reasoning, (the bodies) do not remain with the breath. By this, they show that they want to elude the resurrection of the body, although the divine Scriptures and the very nature of creatures continually testify to the resurrection of the body.

But they say: If the body were not mortal, how could it have happened that, for a small transgression, it had fallen under (the blow of) death, and that the Creator had not had pity on it and forgiven the transgression?

Forgiving and merciful is the Creator, this is evident to all; especially according to (this circumstance, namely) that: after the transgression of man, the incorporeal being having descended, like a corporeal being, made the sound of his footsteps heard in Paradise, and with a sweet and pitiful said to the prevaricator: * Where are you, Adam? lest by seizing him he should not leave him the means to think of penance; and, as (Adam) did not come to his senses, he incurred death precisely as a penalty.

Yet another (argument is) that his (Adam's) Creator had previously given him this injunction: * The day you eat of the fruit of this tree, you die; and his enemy (the enemy of Adam) having afterwards appeared, said: * You do not die, but like God you become. Now, of whose words should we be assured, (the words) of him who previously protected Adam and, by his docility to the commandment, wanted to keep him alive; or (well) the words of the other who, through deception, strove to make (Adam) mortal?

If the Creator, after the transgression of his commandment, had not made man mortal, man would constantly believe Satan and not God; for this one (God) said: * If you eat of this fruit, you die; and he (Satan) said: * If you eat of it, you do not die, but like God you become.

Therefore, death was imposed on the nature of man by the very creator of his nature, so that the word (of God) might be confirmed, and the evil counselor would find himself condemned; for, although for a time, because of these two reasons, (man) has fallen under (the blow of) death, (God), according to his power will resurrect him, and continually in eternity will keep him alive and immortal. He who, having made the angels and the souls of men from nothing, preserves them alive and immortal, he was capable of preserving our body full of life, if the first man had not rejected the order of God.

REFUTATIONS

19. But God is not the cause of death, (this is what) testifies the wise man par excellence, who says that: * God did not cause death, and does not rejoice in the destruction of men ; but God established man in the indestructibility of the image of his eternity, and, through the tempter's jealousy, death entered the world; then (God) himself said: * I said that you were gods, and all sons of the Most High; that is to say, I have made you immortal, if you remain (faithful) to my command; but, since you have not remained (faithful) to my command, as men you die, as one of the princes you fall. I didn't want you dead, nor did I want you to fall in with the bad prince (your) advisor.

But finally, they say, has (God) put them (Satan and man) in conflict with each other?

By this they want to annihilate the free will of Satan and of man; because God who, without jealousy, made them independent, did not want them, like the brutes, to be led by necessity, and then their independence would no longer have been independence.

But God, although he had the power to see the steps of his creatures, did not incite them to fall one on top of the other. When he saw Satan inflamed with jealousy, he let this independent being fight with an independent being; for (God) knew that the independence (or free will) of this one is not weaker than (the independence) of that one. This one does not have foreknowledge, and this one does not have foreknowledge; this one is not (of a) tyrannical force, and this one without power. As (Satan) was not (of a) tyrannical (or irresistible) force, hence it is evident that, having approached the woman with deceit, he questioned her and did not frighten her with violence; and as he did not have foreknowledge, he said: * What did God say to you? in order to learn from her the circumstances.

Then again, from the trials of Job, we can learn that Satan has neither tyrannical force nor foreknowledge; for if he were of a tyrannical (force), he would not seek God, he would not take help, and then he would push (his victims) into temptations; and, if he had foreknowledge, he would not come to attempt, for he would know that when he cannot overcome, he must be (covered) with shame.

Furthermore, from the very temptations of the Lord, we must understand that (Satan) does not have foreknowledge, by the very fact that he said: * If you are the Son of God, he thus showed that, although he had learned from the prophets that the Son of God was to come, he did not know the time of his coming. If he had known that the Son of God was precisely the one who appeared to him as a human (being), he would not have tempted him and would not have been covered with shame, he Satan, who, although after the divine miracles he understood the coming of the Son of God, full of trouble exclaimed: * I know that you are the Holy One of God.

Then again, if he had had any prescience, he would not have incited the Jews to put (Jesus) on the cross; for he would have known that the death of Christ would throw him, (him, Satan, fallen) from his power: according to what the Lord said: * The prince of this world will be thrown out, and then: * I saw Satan as lightning falling from the heavens; then again: * The prince of this world is from now on condemned, to show that (fallen) from his power has fallen the one who wanted to become God, (and that he) has become passive of eternal judgments.

20. Now, since concerning death and pain imposed on man, it has been proven, according to the books given by God himself (the Bible), that because of the transgression of the commandments of God, (death and pain) have entered the world, we will say other causes for which premature deaths occur.

Many times perhaps immense evils stand before man, or anguishes which he cannot endure, or trials which he is not capable of enduring; Prescient and human God, then having pity on his creature, by premature death delivers man from his evils, according to what Scripture says: * Before the wicked will be collected the righteous; then yet another reason: Premature deaths happen so that, at every age and at all times, man, (to be) found prepared, does not free himself from the worship of God.

REFUTATIONS

But although, according to the curse (of God), sorrows have entered into the world, yet there are still other causes; sometimes (they happen) because of sins, according to what the Lord said to the paralytic: * You have been healed, from now on do not sin. Having regard to the faith of those who come near (to him), the Lord said to another paralytic: * Let your sins be forgiven you, to show that there are sorrows which come because of sins, and that there are also sorrows which come not because of sins, as when his disciples asked the Lord concerning the blind man: * Whose sin is it, because of his blindness, of him or of his parents? and (the Lord said: * Neither of him nor of his parents; but (it is) for the glory of God, that God may be glorified in him. There are also sorrows which (occur), not because of sins, and not for the glory of God, but (which result) from the unbalanced mixtures; for the body of man is mixed with four elements, damp, dry, cold and hot. If there is a decrease or an increase, (it) produces pain in the body; and this comes from eating or drinking too much, or from austere fasts, or from choice foods, or from too much heat in working, or from an excess of cold, or other opposites of this kind, by the effect of which these disorders are produced in the bodies.

The beginning of the fighting came from the avarice of men, hence the invasion of borders, foreign villages and towns, goods and possessions.

Likewise, also lust (occurred) for not having kept within the bounds of marriage, which God instituted from the beginning (saying:) * A man will leave his father and his mother and will go after his wife; after his wife, says (God,) and not after women. To confirm the first rule of nature, the Lord said in the holy Gospels: * What God has joined together, let not man separate!

The attacks of the devil come because of the pride of men; for if a son is wise, he does not receive caning, and if he is not wise, many times a caning is applied to a slave in front of him, so that, seeing this, he becomes wise; but, if by this very fact he is not yet amended, the punishment is applied to himself.

21. This has been said concerning the questions of some: If sinners, because of their sins, are tormented by demons, as for innocent children, why do demons rule over them?

God calls all men to adoption, as he said through (the mouth of) his prophet: * My eldest son Israel; then: * I have fathered and raised my sons. If virtuous men under the (Judaic) law were called sons, how much more those to whom (God said) he * gave power to become sons of God!

Now, when God approaches us, his children, to warn us, sometimes he strikes before us, like (in the example of) the slave, our animals, and sometimes our fields and our vineyards, so that, in seeing this, we entered under the yoke of the fear of God; then, if by this we are not yet (sufficiently) warned, (God) applies torments to ourselves, whether by (means) pains, afflictions or demons; the innocent are also tormented, so that others may remember in their minds these words of the wise, who says: * If the righteous barely lives, where will the impious and the sinner be found? And this also happens that the righteous may not fail in righteousness, and that the sinner may not always remain in sin; God is not guilty of this, but the wickedness of men leads God to warn men through these torments; as, through (the means of) the faith of others, he restored the paralytic and granted him forgiveness of his sins; so also by the torments of some, (God) brings to fear and reform many men, when it happens (by means) of the innocent, and when it happens (by means) of sinners, as the only supreme sage himself knows. (It is) not for the condemnation of souls that the torments of demons come to man, but (it is) much more as a result of the mercy (of God), especially if he is an innocent (who is stricken), (it is) to throw fear into the minds of others (that) he is delivered up to these torments, that, like a torch hanging in a large house, shows the providence of God, so that , seeing this, many collect themselves and enter in fear under (the yoke of) the obedience of God.

It sometimes happens that, even because of sins, these torments occur; sometimes also it happens that these terrible blows approach, and that, taking refuge in the relics of the holy martyrs, men are saved from these torments, by

REFUTATIONS

which the power of God which is in his saints appears, and (men) n 'experience no damage themselves.

But the devil does not cast out the demon, this is what (Jesus) Himself made evident. * If Satan, he says, casts out Satan, then he is divided, separated from himself; but I, says (Jesus), by the Spirit of God cast out demons; and why did he who was God, he said, by the spirit of God cast out demons? (it was) to teach men that, if they do not make themselves worthy of the graces of the Holy Spirit, they cannot cast out demons, like the apostles, when they had not received the power of the Lord, could not cast out demons; moreover, even to him who is in torment, (God) has given the power to cast out demons. (The Lord) said: * This (accursed) race only comes out through (the means of) fasting and prayer; not that there is a certain kind of demons that comes out through fasting and prayers, and others not, but all the legions of demons go away, put to flight by fasting and prayers.

22. But sorcerers, they say, send out demons, and cast out demons.

Enchanters cannot cast out demons; To convince us of this, it is enough to have this word from the Lord, who says that: * Satan does not cast out Satan; for if the enchanter cast out (the demons), he would therefore cast them out with the demons, and of the demon Christ said that: * The demon does not cast out the demon; then it is obvious that things happen differently, as (proves) this word coming from them and not from us, they say: (The enchanters) cannot chase (the demon), but they can chain him, so that the demon is constantly there to strangle the souls of men. And this happens precisely according to the judgments of God; for someone has left God, the saints, the fasts, the prayers, and has taken refuge in the enchanter, who cannot help himself; for who among the enchanters is inaccessible to pain, exempt from demons, immortal? What's more, we even see enchanters always exhausted by demons, and especially crisiaques; for first they themselves are taken by the devil, and then they promise to others to give (them) what is neither in their power nor (in the power) of the demons, by whose language they speak of giving, but (that which is in the power) only of God who is the creator, the giver (of all things).

Now, for enchanters, rather than chaining the demon and making it like a shoelace ready to constantly strangle the souls of man, it would be better if (the demon) appeared, than through (the intercession of) saints praying to God, they found help to cure their illness.

But we say that (the demon) does not have the power to enter into man without God's permission, and for this there are several reasons, as only he himself knows; and this is evident from the very fact that when * (the demons) decided to enter a herd of swine, they could not enter until they had first received the order from Christ; and, * when Satan wanted to tempt Job, he could not do so until he had first received the order from God to tempt; and the Lord said of Judas that *Satan entered through a cleft; for if Christ had not allowed it to Satan who pressed him, and to Judas who, because of his avarice, came to this point, (the demon) could not enter into him; but, to reproach them both (Satan and Judas) for their free will, (the Lord) let them do so, according to their will both.

Moreover, when some are still tormented by the devil, if the eye of God were not upon him, he would exterminate them by the cruelest death; and even if God did not firmly guard their servants, they would cripple them in every way, and they would be destroyed by the most terrible death. But, because they are not free to act, they cannot do such things. From there, it is obvious that, although God knows in advance that such an individual must be an idolater, such another an enchanter, such another assassin, he does not prevent the tracing of their embryo, and the insufflation of their soul, so that its goodness is manifested, and that (these people) are condemned in their own free will.

And it is evident that, as (God) is the master of (the action of) doing, so also (he is the master) of making people find pleasure in means, and of saving from the embraces of evil; for (for) him who is his, (God) preserves and cares for him, and (for) him who is not his, (he treats) him as a stranger, cuts him up, scatters him, as he says in the Gospel that: The wolf does not come for anything else, except to ravish and scatter. But as for true believers, Satan cannot subjugate them by his temptations, nor enchanters (subdue them) by demons; as the Lord himself said to his disciples: I have given you power to tread down serpents and scorpions, and all power over the enemy; and then (he said): * These are the signs of the believers: they will cast out demons, and they will take serpents in their hands, and they will drink drugs of death, and (all this) will not harm them. It is said at the same time that: demons cannot harm the innocent, that wild beasts are not inclined to devour him, as to * Daniel the wild beasts did no harm, nor to the three children the fire of the furnace.

As with the first man, when he had not yet transgressed, (the wild beasts) were obedient and not evil; and as, by (means of) the apostles, Satan was mistreated, to the point that * the enchanters, for fear of the miracles that (the apostles) performed, hastened to bring the most precious books of their witchcraft, and to burn before the apostles; and the demons cry out: * These are the servants of the Most High God: remnants of their miracles still appear today in the holy bishops and the true cenobites. (This) whose experience is known, (not only) to Christians, but also to pagans and magi.

23. But we also must know that angels and demons, and the souls of men, are incorporeal; for, of the angels he says: * He made his angels spirits, and his servants flame of fire: he calls them spirits because of their velocity, as if to say that: they are lighter than the winds; for, of (spirit or) breath and of wind, the Hebrew, and Greek, and Syrian name, is the same; so it is found in Armenian, if you pay attention. When someone is strongly pressed by another, he says: he did not give me (time to) breathe a breath; and by this he indicates the air that we suck; and (God) calls the angels (beings) fiery, because of their impetuosity; as elsewhere he says: They are strong in the power to do his will. But it is not that they are of the nature of wind and fire; for if they were of the nature of wind and fire, then they would rightly be called corporeal and not incorporeal; for that which is corporeal is composed of four elements, like the bodies of men and brutes; and that which is incorporeal is a simple nature, like that of angels and demons, and of the souls of men.

And where then will they be able to breathe (these beings, because) they say that the angels married women; for these (the angels) are called igneous and men grasses; from which it is evident that there is no marriage between fire and grass, but absorption. These three series of beings, as being of the same nature, are also called by the same name. Angel is said to be a spirit, but an obligatory spirit, who is obedient and executes the wishes (of the master). Demon is also called a spirit, but a wicked spirit, because of his disobedience and his rebellion. Although in our language, we call it an evil genius, as according to the distinctions of our first fathers, following the custom established among us; but we know that this genius is wind, and the wind is spirit, according to the previous assertion; for we say that the zephyr blows; the Syrians say: the genius blows; and because of their extension only and their rapidity, angels and demons, and the souls of men, are called aerial, that is to say windy; as because of their impetuosity, angels are called igneous; likewise also because of their velocity and their extension (they are called spiritual), that is to say windy; but their nature is above the wind, above the fire, more delicate, more swift than intelligence.

And there is nothing surprising if these (that is to say the angels) are named after creatures, our neighbors, since their creator does not blush to take these names himself. due to certain reports. God is called spirit, but he is a superiority of spirit; it is said: God is spirit, that is to say, vivifying; it is also called fire, according as thy God is a consuming fire. Now let us see if God is only the fire that consumes. Behold, this spirit, by another prophet, is declared light, according to what (is said) that: * The Lord is my light and my life, whom shall I fear?

If (God) were only the consuming fire, how would he be called life-giving light? Is it not evident, then, that where ardor is useful, there it is called fire; and where gentleness (is useful), there (it is called) life-giving light; that is to say, he is above the fire and above the light. Many other names it still takes, because of different properties.

And, when (God) wanted to appear to his saints, never in any other form, but only in the form of man whom he made in his image, he manifested himself; and this was not done in vain, but above all to show the love he had for man, then also to predispose men to the knowledge (of God), so that when he sent his Son as man in this world, we do not regard (this event) as a strange thing, especially so that we know that he himself manifested himself in this form; as: *

having descended into Paradise near Adam, (God) made (hear) the sound of his footsteps, like man, — having come near Abraham with two angels, he found it good to eat in his tent, — and, having reached the mountain with Abraham, he sent his two young men, the angels transformed into men, to Sodom, to his beautiful inn, near Lot, — and, making shine like fire and lightning, his angel in the bush, having trained him in human language, he made him speak with the man already consecrated to God, with Moses, — and, having transformed his general Michel into a hero, he showed him in the plain to his captain Joshua, — and, having sent an angel to the house of Manue to speak with him, he presented him in the manner of men, — and often also (God), almost made man, spoke mouth to mouth, hand in hand, with his friend, with Moses, — * and the man-king having been found according to his heart, being overwhelmed with the blows (of adversity), an angel, under human form, sword in hand, appeared to him, — and to Ezekiel, under the appearance of fire and a tongue of flame, in a chariot drawn by different specters, he made the driver appear in human form, — and he -even, sometimes like an old man, sometimes like a young man, for different intentions, transforming himself, he appeared to the favored man; and, by thus showing himself to his servants, (God) manifested the love he had for man.

All this has been said to show that everything that appears is corporeal, and everything that does not appear is incorporeal; and of corporeal beings, there are some which are heavy in body; there are some which are thin (and light) bodies; as the apostle says that: Others are the bodies of celestial beings, and others (are) the bodies of terrestrial beings; terrestrial, that is to say, men and brutes, birds and reptiles; and of the celestial beings, (i.e.) of the sun and the moon, and of the stars; and then he speaks (of these beings), and not of the angels, bringing back to them the discourse (of the Apostle): One is the glory of the sun, and another the glory of the moon.

At the same time, it is also said that: whatever, of sentient beings, is palpated, examined, felt, all of this is corporeal; and everything among sentient beings that is not felt is incorporeal. Unbound is the element of light; but as by the eye it is examined, it is corporeal. Unbound is the element of air; but, as through the cold it is felt by the body, it is corporeal. Unbound is the element of fire; but, as through heat it is felt by the body, it is corporeal; so also the element of water, which is more subtle than that which is heavy, and heavier than that which is light.

24. Now as incorporeal are the angels and the demons; for this very reason, there is no lineage for them; but they say, mermaids have offspring, and die.

First, let us see this: whether there are any reasonable creatures other than angels, demons and men, and then let us come to consider this (question) of demons. Is there a corporeal part and an intangible part; for there is no rational creature outside of these three species, namely: angels, demons and men; from the divine Scriptures, and from the very nature of creatures, this is evident. But, although some names of onocentaurs, or mermaids, or monsters are mentioned in Scripture, (it is) according to the opinion of the imagination of men and not according to nature, that these nouns occur; for it is the property of demons to assume different forms, and men, according to these forms, impose names. As when cities and villages will be destroyed, and demons will dwell there, and they will appear in different disguises; and men, according to their disguises, imposing names on them, will call one (of these demons) a centaur, another monster, then another mermaid; similarly also Scripture, according to the opinion of men, to signify the intensity of the ruin of the world, says that the * onocentaurs dwell in these ruins, (animals) which the Greek language calls onocentaurs (it is i.e. donkey-bull).

Now let them show that there are bull-donkeys in Babylon. It is therefore evident that without (application to) individuals are found the names of centaurs and onocentaurs; and Scripture, according to the custom of men's opinion, will also have used these names to signify the ruin of Babylon; like the sea bull which is said to be the product of a cow, and the satyr from men, and the licker from a dog. These are not human beings, but imaginary names, and the nonsense of spirits led astray by demons; for from a corporeal being nothing invisible results, just as from an invisible being (does not result) a corporeal being. Never from men came the satyr, who would be a creature with a human face, and (never) from the cows came a marine bull, who would live in the lakes, because for (an earthly being) it is not possible to live in the waters, just as it is not possible for an aquatic being to live on dry land; and from the dog there came (no being) who lives endowed with inapparent powers, and who, when a wounded man falls in combat, heals him by licking him, this is what they call licker. But all this is fables, old wives' tales, and above all produces the fury of demons.

25. But, still discussing these points, they become more and more assertive. One says that: in our village a sea bull made a cow and we constantly hear all its bellows. Another said: I saw a satyr with my own eyes.

As for the licker, can anyone also say that he saw one; and if in the early days the lickers licked the wounded and made them well, why now do they no longer lick and heal? Are these not the same battles and likewise are there no more wounded people?

But then, they say, there were demigods. And we, on the subject of the dives, we will imperiously ask them: Were these dives corporeal or incorporeal? If they were corporeal, it is obvious that they were men, and that, taking these ghosts of men as their object of worship, they were called dives. If they were incorporeal, it was not possible for incorporeal beings to marry corporeal women; because if it were possible, Satan would never stop procreating satanic (beings) with women. He who is incorporeal is without sperm, because sperm is the property of corporeal (beings), and not of incorporeal (beings); and, without sperm being born of a woman, this was only possible for a single being, who is the creator of the nature of the body, and as he wanted, he could be born of a virgin, without the (means of) marriage.

From which (it follows that) all the profane sages, considering the impotence of each of these dives, could not say that from a woman someone (among them) was born without the (help of) marriage. And as there is no offspring for the dives, so also there is no death. Although immortal by nature is only the Divinity which is eternal, and not (that) taking from someone the beginning of being, but to beings having beginning, to rational beings, (God) gave immortality, I mean to angels and demons, and also to the souls of men. Among these beings, men, because they are (composed) of the two natures, (of the nature) of corporeal (beings) and (of that) of incorporeal (beings), propagate by (way of birth), and come to the propagation (of the species) by (means of) marriage. They die by the body and not by the soul, because of the transgression (of the first man).

But angels and demons receive neither increase by birth, nor decrease by death; but as they were instituted, so also, they remain in the same number, without increase or decrease, and there is no other creature that can come into different forms, as is published concerning the dragons and monsters of rivers. But (it is) only angels and demons who can travel through the air, explore it, and affect different forms.

But dragons, they say, and river monsters appear in different guises. One of them is in the state of individual, the other in the non-individual state.

The dragon, which is a corporeal being, cannot change its forms; for if it were possible for corporeal beings to change their forms, first of all man who is more than them (dragons and river monsters) would change his forms into those he wanted. But as it is not possible for man to change (his forms) into whatever forms he wishes, so also (it is not possible for the dragon).

Furthermore, there is no monster in the state of non-individual, except that the demon has lived in (some) places, and that sometimes it has transformed itself, and sometimes it has committed damage. Dragons do not carry their household (with them) and they do not have beasts of burden which carry it to them from their lodging elsewhere; It is absurd to say to an individual: Stick to your lodging all the time and don't take another one; for the dragon who is himself a beast of burden, by the very fact that he is (in the state of) brute and non-speaking, how could he who is a beast of burden govern another beast of burden? for the dragon has no other nature than that of the serpent; this is obvious: the enormous serpent, or some sea beast, the Scriptures call dragon; like the invincible man they call him giant; so also the monstrous terrestrial serpent, and every sea beast having the shape of a mountain, I say the whales and the dolphins, they call it dragons, according to (what is said): * That you have broken the heads of the dragons on the waters, and you gave them as food to the Ethiopian people.

Do you see? that: the great fish of the sea, the Scriptures call dragons. This is evident from what they say about the fish: You gave them as food to the Ethiopian nations. Although here others have represented the dragon in Satan, as what Job wrote shows; dragons are not something else, except enormous terrestrial serpents or monstrous marine fish. (It is of them) that the Scriptures say that: They are high as mountains and of excessive grandeur. Their hunting and their food are small fish, like (the hunting and food of) snakes, these are the small animals or brutes; but not hunting like (that which) men have done to dragons, or even will do. They have no palace as men for habitation, they have none of the princes of royal blood, nor of the heroes chained near them living; for there are none living among corporeal beings but two (individuals) Enoch and Elijah.

But, as with Alexander, the demons deceived by saying that: he will remain alive; these, according to Egyptian invention, having chained and thrown the demon into a vial by incantations, made people believe that Alexander was alive and seeking death; and the coming of Christ confounded this imposture and removed this scandal; in the same way also the curse of the demons deceived the followers of the cult of heroes in Armenia (into believing) that an (individual) named Ardavazt is a prisoner of the demons, (Ardavazt) who until now is alive, but must escape and possess the world; thus the infidels remain attached to a vain hope; like the Jews who cling to vain expectation, (believing that) David must come and build Jerusalem and gather the Jews, and reign over them.

And thus, Satan strives to frustrate every man of good hope, and to attach him to a vain hope. He glorifies dragons in the eyes of men, so that, when they appear terrible to some, they may take them as (objects of) worship. (Satan) makes people believe that there would be river monsters and plains spirits, and, after having persuaded this, (Satan) transforms himself into a dragon or a river monster and a spirit, in order thereby to divert the man of his Creator; for if there were some (river) monster in the personal state, it would not sometimes appear in the form of a woman and would not sometimes be a seal, and would not swallow up the swimmers who fell under its feet. But where woman, woman he would stand, or seal, seal he would remain.

Likewise also, what they call genius of the plains, would not appear sometimes man, and sometimes serpent, (means) by which it was imagined to introduce the cult of the serpent into the world. Likewise also, he would not appear once in the form of a serpent, and another time in the form of a human; as previously it was said that whatever is corporeal in other forms cannot change.

But if mules and camels appear in the threshing floors, these are demons and not dragons; and if on the plains, fast-running beasts, riding like men, rush after game, this is a surprise of demons; This is the pretense of demons, and not the truth of (real) things, and if something appears in the rivers in the form of women, it is the transformation of Satan; for there is no river monster in the personal state, and the dragon does not enter man as a demon, as some have thought from the exclamations of the possessed man; for to a corporeal (being), into a corporeal being it is not possible to enter. Even if such a dragon were to rise in the air, (it would not be) by means of oxen, but by some hidden power according to the command of God, lest the breath of the dragon harm man or the brute, like this species of serpent, which is called basilisk, by its gaze alone exterminates the man or the brute. Hence (it happens that), when it is found in the wells, they go down there with a light to catch the serpent, so that, looking at the light, it does no harm to the man.

26. But we, according to the holy books, know the angels appointed to help men, nations and kingdoms, according to what is said that: * He established the states of the nations according to the number of the angels of God, and then by what (God) says in the Gospel: Do not despise one of the little ones; for their angels always see the face of my Father who is in heaven. Thus, it seems that to each man remains (attached) a guardian angel. Although others have thought concerning the prayer uttered by the Lord, that their prayers which continually come before God, are called angels; but the apostle says: * Are not all spirits necessary envoys (attached) to the service of those who are to possess salvation? These beings, who are appointed to this office, become for us auxiliaries of salvation.

27. But, if Satan is, they say, the instigator of evils, to other creatures why does he offer the cult of paganism and does not take it up for himself?

For Satan is accused of wickedness, this is evident to all. Now, if he alone demanded worship, he would quickly terrify his worshipers by the very fact that he would appear to them to be wicked and persecuting. But he has disposed half (of men) to worship the stars, and the rest (to worship) air and fire, earth and water, and substances, and woods and stones, even to the snakes and wild beasts, and animals, in order only to satisfy his hatred (and the desire) that he took it into his head to attack man. Therefore, let not those who worship creatures triumph, (by saying) that they do not do the will of Satan; for, of the worship rendered to creatures, there is no other teacher and master than Satan alone.

Now how can they curse Satan, those who do his will? and, if those who cultivate the true God, and are lost by their conduct, are confounded by the divine language (which says that): * They promise to know God, and by their works they deny him; how many more remain without responding, those who, having received the worship of the true (God), offer (adoration) to inanimate and mute creatures!

28. But, although with different weapons the enemy of the truth is provided, by making the wise men of Greece think that a matter always stood near God, (matter) from which he (drew and) made the creatures; and, as the name of matter, in their language, is close to mud, because of this, they thought that from (matter) came the beginning of evils.

The inventors of the Persian religion, having doubted where evils come from, by the same routes, strayed far from the truth, stammered the same nonsense with other stories, pretending that from one father two children were born, one good and creator of good, the other evil and artisan of evil. Into the same trap have also fallen the sects which * the enemy, like tares, has sown among the wheat; because some (of these sects) admitted three roots (or principles, that of) good, (that of) righteousness, and (that of) evil. The others (admitted) two (principles, that) of good and (that) of evil. Still others admitted seven (principles).

Now, this is the work of the Church of God: to confound the profane (or infidels) by the realities of the truth, without (the help of) the Scriptures, and, as for the opinions of believers not conforming to the truth, the correct, with the help of holy books.

As for the material opinions in which the Greeks were lost, we believe we have sufficiently reached them through this first treaty, but, against the inventors of the Persian religion, (after having) taken refuge in the graces of God, we will enter into struggle.

BOOK TWO
REFUTATION OF THE RELIGION OF THE PERSIANS

1. While there was yet nothing, they say, neither heavens nor earth, nor any other creatures which are in the heavens or (on the) earth, there was one named Zerouan, (word) which is translated: fate or glory. A thousand years he made sacrifice, so that a son might come to him, whose name (would be) Ormizt, who made the heavens and the earth, and all that is therein, and, after a thousand years of sacrifices made, (Zeruan began to think, and said: Of what use will be the sacrifice that I make? Will there come to me a son Ormizt, or will I finally make an effort? And while he was still thinking this, Ormizt and Arhmèn were sent (or conceived) in the womb of their mother. Ormizt, according to the sacrifice made, and Arhmèn, according to the doubt (expressed); then informed (of this), Zerouan said: Two sons are here in this womb Whoever of (among) them comes first to me, I will make him king; and Ormizt, having known the thoughts of his father, revealed (them) to Arnhèn. He said: Zerouan, our father, thought that whoever of us comes to him first, he will make him king. Having heard this, Arhmèn pierced (his mother's) womb, and went to present himself before his father; and having known it, Zerouan did not know who he was, and he asked: Who are you? and he (Arhmèn) said: I am your son. (But), said Zérouan, my son has a sweet smell, and luminous, and you, you are dark and stinking. And while they were still talking among themselves, Ormizt, having been born at his time, luminous, and with a sweet smell, came to present himself before Zérouan; and, having seen him, Zerouan knew that he was his son Ormizt, for whom he was making sacrifices; and having taken the rods that he had in his hand, he gave (them) to Ormizt, and said: * Until now, for you, I made sacrifices; from this moment on, you will do some for me; and, giving him the wands, Zerouan to bless Ormizt. Arhmèn having (then) presented himself before Zérouan, said to him: * Have you not thus taken an oath? whoever of my two sons comes first to me, will I make him king? And Zérouan, to evade his wish, said to Arhmèn: Oh! be false and evil, let you be given a reign of nine thousand years, and I will make Ormizt king over you, and after nine thousand years Ormizt will reign, and whatever he wants to do, he will do it. Then Ormizt and Arhmèn began to make creatures, and

whatever Ormizt did was good and right, and whatever Arhmèn did was evil and tortuous.

2. To these impious speeches, to these nonsense of ignorant, fantastic minds, there was no need to respond at all; for sufficient was their ineptitude to confound them, (and to confound the falsity) of their words which clash with one another, and are contrary to one another. But, as by this very fact, the leaders of their religion appear in great esteem to those who obey them, and, throwing (so to speak) the rope over them, drags them into the abyss, it is necessary to give an answer, and show that (these leaders) say nothing more than (what) Mani said, which they themselves have excoriated.

For he (Mani) says (that there are) two roots, (one) of good and (the other) of evil, and that not by projection and birth, but existing in themselves and contrary l 'one to the other; and these (the magi) say the same thing, (as produced) by the desires of Zerouan by means of projection and birth; and, if it is the same religion on both (sides), why do the Magi hate the sectarians (of Mani), if it is not that they are separated from each other by morals, although (it is) by the forms and not by reality? But, in one and the same religion, there are two (parties); these admit two roots, and these likewise; these worshipers of the sun, and these servants of the sun; these attribute breath to every inanimate thing, and these think in the same way.

But Mani wanted to feign morals more excellent than theirs, as if he were completely free from passions, from (carnal) desires, not more than them only, but also more than (the believers of) all religions, hence (it happened that), having been accused of seduction (towards) young girls, he was deprived of life by a (cruel) death, he was flayed. From this it is evident that only by morals are separated from each other (the Persians and the Manichaeans).

3. Now, leaving these, we will ask these: Was Zerouan, whom they say was prior to everything, perfect or imperfect? If they say that he was perfect, let them hear this: If he were perfect, then did he need to ask anyone for a son, who would come and make heaven and earth? for if he were perfect, he himself was

able to make the heavens and the earth; then, if he was imperfect, it is evident that there was someone above him, who could fill (the void of) his imperfection; and if he were someone above him, it was necessary for that someone to make the heavens and the earth, and everything that is there, to show his beneficence and his power, and not to grant to Zeroan a son who makes the heavens and the earth, and everything that is therein.

But, they say, he made a sacrifice for glory.

We will ask: whose glory had come to him? since he was eternal, he was glorified. If glory was given to him by anyone, we must think that there was someone above him, more powerful and more glorious, from whom the glory came to him. Then, if there was no one above him, it was in vain to make age-old sacrifices; for glory is not in the state of person; but, according to the happiness of an individual, we say glory, just as, according to the misfortune of an individual, we say adversity; and these two (states) are products of accidents, and not constitutions of persons.

Another (thing) still; for if the sun and the moon were not yet produced, (those stars) by which the hours, and the days, and the months, and the years are regulated, (this account of) a thousand years, from which appeared- he ? for there were no stars in space which regulate the number of days, and months, and years; but it is obvious that this nonsense is full of nonsense.

Then again, if the heavens and the earth and what is there were not, where (so Zerouan) did he sacrifice? or, with what? When the earth did not exist, nor the plants which (come) from it, where did he find (to draw) wands to have in his hand, or what did he sacrifice then, since the brutes were not still trained? And what is more stupid than all (the rest), a thousand years, they say, he made a sacrifice, and after a thousand years he doubted and said: * Will Ormizt happen to me, or will it not happen- shall I not, and shall I labor in vain? and through this, (Zérouan) shows that Zérouan was powerless, needy and without knowledge. The cause of evils is himself and not Arhmèn; for if he (Zeruan) had not doubted, as they say, Arhmèn would not have happened, (Arhmèn) whom they proclaim the creator of evils; but he doubted, which is incredible and full of confusion.

For never from a single (and the same) source come two streams, one sweet and the other bitter; nor from one and the same tree two fruits, one sweet and the other sharp. Now, if (as) sweet they recognize Zerouan, they should not think that a bitter fruit, Arhmèn, came out of him; and if they consider (Zeruan) to be bitter, there is no reason to admit (as coming from) a sweet fruit, Ormizt. Thus suits them the divine language, which says: * Or make the tree sweet, and its fruit sweet also; or make the bitter tree and its bitter fruit; for from the tree its fruit is known.

And if the creatures each remain in their (state) of formation, and never exceed the limits assigned to them, how much more Zerouan, if he were an immortal being, and sought the means to make creatures, either through himself- even, whether by others, or by his son, as they say, should show some order and not disorder and confusion!

For we have never seen that cows gave birth to donkeys, nor donkeys to oxen, nor wolves to sheep, nor sheep to foxes, nor lions to horses, nor horses to snakes. But only there is a propagation that men have invented outside the rules of nature, (propagation which consists of) giving birth to mules (from mating) horses and donkeys; and these (products or mules) are without sperm and without generation; for they were not established by God, but by the invention of men. Now, Zerouan, if he were an ox, how would he generate the scorpion Arhmèn? and, if he were a wolf, how would he father the lamb Ormizt? Are these not the follies of human imagination?

Because Zérouan is made a man, a famous character among the Titans. As the Greeks, the Ariks and all the nations of the pagans are accustomed to taking the brave for sons of gods; considering (from this point of view) the head of the religion of the Persians, since the men of this country hold him to be God, I, as to the very creation of the heavens and the earth, and of all creatures, I will suppose (that they make it emanate) from him.

REFUTATIONS

And, as true is this discourse, from this it is evident that (Zoroaster) institutes his religion in the human way, and that by (way of) engenderment and birth he composes this religion; for first he publishes as (coming from) a single father the births of two creators, (namely the one) of good and (the one) of evil, and then, by (way of) incest with the mother and with the sisters, he introduces the creature of the stars, and this not for anything else, except because of sensuality and pleasant concupiscence; for, having regard to the nation of the Arik, (seeing) that they were inclined to women, therefore propitious to these inclinations, he combined his laws, so that, when (the Arik) hear say of their gods that they have indulged in infamous mixtures, they too, resembling them, commit indiscriminately the same turpitudes, which is far removed from the Divinity who is on high; for God, (to) have a son, does not use marriage; but (he has this Son) from all eternity, like the reason of intelligence, the flow of the source, the heat of the fire, the luminous action of the sun; and not, as they assure, that Zerouan needed a son to be born to him, whose name would be Ormizt.

Oh stupidity! No son present anywhere, and (Zérouan) imposed a name on who was neither conceived nor born; to all children, after their birth only names are imposed, and he (Zérouan), how before the birth (of his son), did he impose the name Ormizt on him? except that he believed that a son would come to him; and, if he believed it, why did he doubt, and was his doubt the cause of the birth of Ahmen? whence (comes) evils entered into the world; and, what is still astonishing, is that one (of the children), after a sacrifice made over a thousand years, was barely produced, the other immediately from doubt (was the result).

Then (he, Zerouan), who knew that two sons were here in the womb (of their mother), why did he not also know this: that one (was) good and the other bad? and if he knew it, and did not destroy the evil (son), he himself is the cause of evil; then, if he did not know it, how is it credible that he knew the other? And if then he did not understand (the truth), when he saw the dark and stinking (Arhmèn), did he not then know it? But he knew it and saw it, and made (this dark being) king; he himself is the cause of evils, by the very fact that he did not annihilate the bad (son), but even gave him a reign of nine thousand years; and over whom did he make him reign, if not over the good creatures produced by Ormizt, to torment them by mixing with them his bad creatures?

But also, as for Ormizt, they say, Zerouan made him reign over Arhmèn.

If Ormizt was his king, how did he give him his good creatures to torment? If the father does not take care of his son's creatures, because he has delivered them into the hands of evil, and the son how does he not take care of his own? (Is it) out of helplessness or out of malice? If, through impotence, he does not preserve them, then now it is not (given) to him to reign, nor even in the end can he conquer, as they say. But, if (it is) out of malice (that he does not preserve his own), it turns out that not only the father, who made the bad son reign, is responsible for the evils, but even his son (Ormizt) who was an accomplice of his father and liberator of the wicked (Arhmèn), or rather the cause of his irruption.

Then, as (Zeruan) gave the kingdom to his sons; to one (for) nine thousand years, and to the other forever, in what order was he (Zeruan)? for while there was yet nothing, he was king of no one, for he was creator of nothing; and when his sons were (born), they were creators, one of good things, and the other of evil, and they were kings, one temporarily and the other eternally; and Zerouan remained deprived (of the power) of creation and kingdom. He is not a creator, because he has done nothing; he was not king, because of what creatures would he be king? And it is obvious that there never was a Zerouan and that there is none; for whoever is someone is either creator or creature. Now, he (Zeruan), as he is neither creator nor creature, never (he was) God, he is not and did not become one.

4. But as Zerouan, they say, thought this in his mind: If one of my children comes to me first, I will make him king, Ormizt knew this and discovered the plan in Arhmèn.

If Ormizt knew his father's thoughts, why did he not know the plan of his perfidious brother, who pierces the belly (of their mother), rushes, and goes

REFUTATIONS

forward to take the kingdom, which unfortunately should have given him happen to him and his creatures? for, first having thrown him back, (Arhmèn) will mistreat (Ormizt), and then, for nine thousand years, (Ormizt) will be afflicted, desolate, as a result of the evil eye cast on his good creatures, that (Arhmèn) will conquer, will corrupt; or Zerouan, who knew of the conception of his two sons in the womb of their mother, when Arhmèn appeared before him, why did he not know him?

Then (Zérouan), who knew his son Ormizt to be of a sweet smell, and luminous from the womb (of his mother), how did he not know that his other son was stinking, and dark? Is it not obvious, then, that these are not certain things which are told by them, but fables and nonsense?

And yet another thing which is more incredible than all, (that is) that one (of the sons), after a sacrifice of a thousand years, was barely produced, the other immediately after doubt came into being. ; and, if according to this doubt the son Arhmèn happened, (Zeruan) should not call him his son; for if he were his son, he was like him, or good, if (his father Zerouan) was good, or bad, if he was bad. Was their father Zerouan also good and bad, and from the good vein came the good son, and from the bad artery (was born) the bad (son)? If it were not so, (Zeruan) would not call the wicked his son and give him the kingdom. But, if (Zeruan) were himself good, he would destroy the wicked, and to the good would give the kingdom; through this he would himself become (worthy of an) illustrious name and would not make his good son Ormizt always sad. But from all this it is evident that there never was a Zerouan, father of the gods, and giver of kingdoms.

5. They also say: The rods that (Zeruan) had in his hand, he gave to his son Ormizt, and said: Until now I have made sacrifices for you, from now on you will make sacrifices for me.

Now, if (Zeruan) made sacrifices for him (Ormizt), so that to him (Zeruan) there might be a son; About whom did Ormizt make sacrifices for Zerouan? Had some suspicion come from somewhere (to Zérouan), and because of this, he had ordered Ormizt to make sacrifices for him? Would the one from whom he requested a son, by giving him this son, take his share? If that was on his mind, wands couldn't help him; and, in giving him these wands, (Zérouan) did not say to Ormizt: You will make sacrifices for me, to show that he was someone to whom he, (Zérouan), for his son made sacrifices, and (Zérouan) ordered his son (Ormizt) to make sacrifices for him to this being.

If there was someone above him (Zeruan) and his son, (someone) to whom they made sacrifices, this someone had to be believed because of (Zeruan and Ormizt), and creator of all, and not (believe) Zerouan cause of Ormizt and Arhmèn, and these creators of evils and goods; (rather) than giving Zerouan a creative son, could not he who was above Zerouan, by himself, make the heavens and the earth and everything that is there, as he was said previously, and show (thus) his power and his beneficence? or, if of his son Arhmèn Zérouan had some suspicion, and because of that gave the wands to Ormizt, so that, by (the virtue of) these wands, in making sacrifices to a superior being, he would be without worry; therefore there had to be someone there to whom he made sacrifices, and, if there was someone there to whom there was an obligation to make sacrifices, then Zerouan was not eternal, but produced by someone, and it was necessary to inquire from whom it came, and who was the one to whom he himself made sacrifices, and who was the one to whom he ordered his son to make sacrifices for him? for it is not possible for someone to take the beginning of being if he does not take (or receive) being from another. And only God could make something out of nothing, as he wants. Therefore, who made Zerouan, except God, to whom (Zerouan) made sacrifices, (God) who gave him such a son, that (this son) might make the heavens and the earth and everything that is there? It is astonishing that he himself did not do (all this), and was able to give the son of Zerouan the (power to) do it.

But there was no one there, they say, to whom Zerouan made a sacrifice: if this is so, Zerouan himself was not there; and it is a thing very worthy of mockery, that whoever was not, to whoever was not, for whoever was not made sacrifices.

6. But if fortune was, as they say, Zeroan, then of someone it was fortune. And who was the one whose fortune it was? for fortune is nothing to the state of any

REFUTATIONS

person, but an accident of prosperity; as of righteousness the righteous is called, and of valor the valiant, so also of glory (is called) fortune. So, if fortune was Zerouan, he was nothing in the state of anyone. From which it is obvious that even he was not Zérouan at all.

And if, as they say, doubt was conceived in Arhmèn, first of all, he (Zérouan) had to doubt, because immediately a son would have come to him, and not wait a thousand years, make sacrifices so that he a son was born. However, it happened to him that good and bad (son, the bad) took his wickedness from his morals, and not from birth itself; for it was not possible for a single womb to receive the maker of evils, and the creator of good; for if (this womb) was bad, only for the wicked it must be the receptacle; and, if it was good, of the good (only) it must be the container; because the good and the bad in the same (matrix) could not happen; as wolves and lambs are not born from the same womb. The side of good, they suppose to emanate from Ormizt, (such as) oxen, sheep and other useful animals; the side of evil, (they attribute it) to Arhmèn, (such as) wolves, wild beasts and harmful animals. They do not know that, as with harmful beings, it is impossible to dwell with harmless beings, so also it was not possible for the good to be conceived in the same womb with the bad; for, for example, it is not possible to make (unite) fire and water in the same point, without the predominant side becoming destructive of its companion, in the same way also for the good and the bad, it does not was not possible to enter the same place; otherwise, either this one corrupted this one, or this one corrupted that one.

Now, if (Ormizt and Arhmèn) were produced from sperm, it was not possible for a single individual to project two sperm contrary to each other. Furthermore, (it was not possible) for the same womb to receive two different sperms; for, although several men approach the same woman, the sperm of all these men do not fight each other; because the first sperm that falls (into the womb) leaves the others as superfluous (and useless), and how could it have happened that this womb received two sperm that are enemies of each other?

And then, why did she not overcome, (her), offspring born of sacrifices, and there came an obstacle to her in the offspring born of doubt? But descended there together, these enemies, with (entirely) peaceful agreement, lounged in the same womb. Moreover, the father, if he knew of two children (enclosed) in this womb, should not rashly promise the kingdom; but he had to (promise it) only to the one for whom he was making sacrifices.

But Ormizt, before he was born, was therefore imperfect; and how, imperfect, did he understand his father's thoughts? because he who can know someone's thoughts, he is above (the other). Which is (the doing) of God and not of man. From which (it follows that) Ormizt is more excellent than his father, (more) strong and (more) wise; for while he was still in the womb, he knew the mind of his father, and came out of that womb; he was (enough) powerful to make the heavens and the earth, which his father could not make.

And now, (Ormizt), who was so strong and so wise, (more) than his father, finds himself more deceived, because he was deceived by the perfidious one, in that he revealed the thoughts of his father to the one with whom he must have had implacable enmity, and not friendship.

Then again, if it was necessary to pierce the mother's womb and get out, it was up to him, (Ormizt), who knew his father's thoughts; for thus, he would be the first (to present himself), and take the kingdom, and not from Arhmèn, who did not know the mind of the father, and was not (destined) for the throne. But, if (Arhmèn) pierced (his mother's) womb, he perhaps even caused his mother to perish. We must inquire whether (Ormizt and Arhmèn) really had a mother.

But how would it be evident that they had a mother, especially because they say that while there was still nothing, neither heaven nor earth, Zerouan alone was? What is very worthy of laughter (is) that: he would be a father, and (he would be) a mother; the same (individual) would have projected the sperm and would have collected it. And what is even more pitiful: When Arhmèn, they say, had pierced the belly (of his mother) and came to present himself before his father, the father did not recognize him. How could he not know him, since there was no one there, when he himself was alone? Was it not obvious then that the one who came to him was one of his children? And there is still one thing more pitiful than the pitiful (proposition above), which is that this one (Arhmèn) knew this one (Zérouan), and this one (Zérouan) did not know that one (Arhmèn), and denied his son, (saying:) My son is of a sweet smell, and bright; and you are dark and stinking; and how was he not her son, the one who with his good son had been conceived in the same womb; and he denied him, (saying:) You are not my son, and recognized the other, (saying:) He is my son. If he denied (Arhmèn) as evil, then he should not find him worthy of conception, but (he should) reject him as evil, and exterminate him, not only him (Arhmèn), but also Ormizt, who revealed (his father's) thoughts.

7. But yet another thing more ridiculous, which they say: it is that (Zérouan) gave his rods to (Ormizt) to make sacrifices in his favor, as if (it was) not in Ormizt or in the the same sacrifice that power was, but in the wands; because, if (Ormizt) had the assurance of being heard, it was superfluous for him to have wands in his hand; and, if he was not worthy, the rods were not (thing) sufficient to make him who was unworthy worthy to make sacrifices; because having (in hand) these rods and making sacrifices is the work of man and not of God. Now, if he (Ormizt) was God, and was (enough) powerful to make the heavens and the earth, what need did he have to have (in hand) these rods, and to make sacrifices to deliver his father from his fears? he (Ormizt) who was powerful enough to make the heavens and the earth without these wands, how could he not reassure his father without these wands? It was therefore evident that the father was foolish, helpless, and seeking support in another, and that the son (was) equally helpless, senseless; for neither he (Zeruan) could father his son without making sacrifices, nor the son, without taking the wands in hand, could free (his father) from his fears.

8. Moreover, to the vexations of evil there were two causes, to torment the good creatures of good; for Ormizt, they say, (all) that was good, he did, and just and beneficent men; and Arhmèn made evil creatures and demons.

Now, if demons were evil creatures and wicked by nature, none of them could ever conceive of anything good, especially Arhmèn. But we see here that, of an object which is even very pleasant among creatures, as they say, Arhmèn was the inventor. When he saw, they say, that Ormizt had made beautiful creatures and that he did not know how to make light, he reflected with the demons, and said: What advantage is there for Ormizt? He made these beautiful creatures, and they dwell in darkness, because he did not know how to shed light. Now, if he were wise, he would enter (in commerce) with his mother, he would throw himself on his sister, and the moon would be born; and he would order that no one reveal his thoughts. Having heard this, Mahmi, demon, quickly went near Ormizt, and revealed this project to him. O ineptitude and insipid stupidity! (Ormizt), who was able to find the means of saving the heavens, the earth, and everything that is there, could not foresee these few means of trickery; and, by this very fact, not only do they make Ormizt foolish, but also (they make) Arhmèn good, author of good creatures.

As they say yet another thing, (namely) that Ahmen said: Not that I cannot do something good, but I do not want to; and, to establish this assertion, he played the peacock. Do you see that he is evil by his will, and not by nature?

Now, what is more brilliant than light, of which Arhmèn was the inventor? or what could be more beautiful than the peacock he made, to show his power to create beauty? and from this it is evident that, however evil by nature Arhmèn was, he would not be the inventor of light, nor the creator of beauty. Moreover, if demons by nature were evil, it would not be possible for Mahmi to foresee the conditions for the creation of light, to which until now the followers of this religion, three times a year, offer sacrifices. From which (it follows that) they are afflicted with the reproach of being, themselves, followers of demons; and demons are not evil by nature, but by will; and if they themselves offer sacrifices to demons, by what power will they drive out the followers of demons? Do you see that all that is said by them are fables and vain stories?

9. Then those who attribute the creation of luminous (bodies) to these causes, circumventing this assertion, introduce another cause of the existence of the sun; Arhmèn, they say, invited Ormizt to a meal; Ormizt having gone there, did not want to eat until their sons had first fought; and the son of Ahmen having slain the son of Ormizt, (the two fathers) looked for a judge, and found none; then they made the sun so that it would become their judge.

REFUTATIONS

There, they say Arhmèn inventor of the being of the sun; here it is evident (that he was only) co-creator of light; and, if there was not some other being there for judge, could they not (Ormizt and Arhmèn) go near their father or near the one to whom the father and the son (Ormizt) made sacrifices according to the fable?

And now, how were they enemies of each other, Ormizt and Arhmèn, they who, in the same womb rested, and went to each other's meals; they who, by mutual cooperation, having created the sun, established it as their judge? Now, first, a certain Zratachd (Zoroaster) attributes (the fact) to libertinage (saying that), from incestuous intercourse with the mother and the sister, the sun and the moon were produced, so that upon seeing this, his nation (that is to say the nation of Zoroaster) indulged without reflection in the same turpitudes. Another time, to hide this shame, Zoroaster publishes that, for the (need of) judgment (Ormizt and Arhmèn) made (the sun), and, as in writing are not (recorded) the religions, sometimes they say that, and by this they deceive, and sometimes (they say) this, and by this very thing they deceive the ignorant. But, if Ormizt were God, out of nothing he could make the stars, like the heavens and the earth, and not as a result of an infamous commerce, or a lack of judge.

10. Then they say yet another thing, which is not at all credible; (they say that:) as Ormizt was dying, he projected his semen into a spring, and near the end, from this semen a virgin was born, and from her a child (issued), defeating many of the troops of Arhmèn ; and two (beings) of the same species having appeared, beat his troops and exterminated them.

First, by this they are confounded; for water is not a preserver of sperm, but (it is) destructive of it; and then, on another point, they are also beaten: rather than giving his sperm to a fountain to keep alive, why could he (Ormizt) not keep himself alive; but son of this good God, by the bad son (Arhmèn) he was exterminated. It is obvious that those who, in their state of abjection, defeated (the) good (Ormizt) and his son, in the end must dominate those who have such innumerable troops.

Then, if their gods are mortal themselves, how will they have hope of the resurrection, and especially of a triple resurrection, which must not be deemed resurrection, but non-resurrection. But if precisely, as they say, his son, (the son of Ormizt) died, affecting Ormizt and his other son Chorached, there was no room for doubt that they would die, since they were of a race of (beings) married and mortal is the house of their gods.

Such gods must be considered not (for) true gods, but (for) false gods; for he who is the true God has (gathered) everything around his eternity; like his essence, likewise, (he has) eternal vitality, and his son, always with him, without cause, without anyone's intermediary. Creation (he holds it) not from some invention, but from his voluntary power; he has no one (who is) contrary to him, (no one other who, while) he would be the creator of goods, (or she), the creator of evils; like them, they attribute the good creatures to Ormizt, and the bad ones to Arhmèn. What they cannot demonstrate, if they look carefully, (is that he is not an) evil creature, who is evil by nature, nor Arhmèn, nor even the demons whom they suppose to be his creatures; as many times, through frequent examples, we did not forget, in our first speech, to demonstrate this.

But, if Arhmèn appears bad to them, because he bears the name of Haraman, for having thrown out of the sun (of life) the followers of the sun, (circumstance) from which he took the name of Haraman; so also the name of Satan is not a name of nature, but of morals, as of goodness one is called good, and of wickedness, evil. It's not that morals are innate, but (they) come (with time). And from this it is evident that many times we see many thoughtless (people) becoming thoughtful, and thoughtful (people) becoming thoughtless; foolish people become sensible, sensible people become foolish. This is what (happens) on the part of reasonable beings.

11. Furthermore, (as for what is) irrational beings, brutes, because of their different morals, we must not believe them to be two creators, as these people, through ineptitude, thought that Ormizt made brutes, quadrupeds, and birds, and fish, and everything that is good and beautiful; and that Ahmen (made) wild beasts and unclean birds, and reptiles, and serpents, and scorpions, and all harmful animals. If the heavens and the earth and the waters of Ormizt were

creatures, how would the harmful beings made by Arhmèn dwell on the land of Ormizt and suck the air, (feed on) the foods that are (taken) from the earth, and in the same waters would grow impure animals with non-impure fish, and in the same air would carnivorous birds circle with the sweetest birds, (evil beings) that Ormizt, (author) of good creatures, had to exterminate and not maintain; for from him are the earth, and the waters, and the air.

And, if wild beasts, because of their evil action, are reputed (to come) from some bad creator, it is more appropriate to believe men (made) by the bad creator, and not animals; for these (that is, men), are more harmful to wild beasts than wild beasts to these; because these (men), leaving the towns and villages, begin to pursue, in order to exterminate them, the wild beasts; and these, (the wild beasts) rush into the mountains and steep places, hasten to throw themselves everywhere fugitives. The dens of most (of these ferocious beasts) are out of the frequentation of men.

Likewise also reptiles perceiving the noise of man alone; there are some who penetrate into holes, who in dens, who in excavations of the earth and lurk; and, if, by pursuing animals too much, men suffer harm, the harm is to men, and not to them (that is to say, to the animals), by this very fact by some bad creator he we should not believe wild beasts and (harmful) animals to be products, but rather created by a single good creator; half for our needs and half for ornament, some (as) a scarecrow to lower the unjust pride of man. Even, looking at their harmful action, we do not see them harming each other; and, if we must hate their evil action, which does not occur through thought, how much more (must we hate) the evil action of men which is exercised through reflection and trickery!

Moreover, by the smallest (beings) (God) makes us torment, as by the flea and by the fly, and by the cousin and by the wasp, and by the mosquito and by the rat, and by others similar (insects) which are animalcules, and can tire us; for there are some among them that weary us, and there are some that are harmful to us, like the rat, the moth and the worm, and others (animals) similar to them. (God), by their means, lowers and depresses (the pride of) our thoughts; because, when we know that such small (animals) can be harmful to us, we will descend (from the height) of unjust pride (for) not having our person in such great esteem.

Then (we must) consider the providence of God; if small (animals) can harm us, how could we live if, with reptiles and wild beasts, (God) had made us cohabitants? But also, to this we must look, (that is) how many brutes (God), for our needs, has subjected us: horses, camels, elephants, herds of oxen and sheep; and, in the mountains and in the plains, deer, stags, wild sheep and wild boars, (all animals) half of which are beasts of burden, and half good for eating.

And (God) has given us to know that over the animals he wants (for us to triumph over), we can become victorious, and (that) over those over which he does not want (to make us victorious), we cannot triumph over, no- only considerable (animals), but even (more) tiny ones. What's more miserable than the flea and the rat? and we cannot exterminate this (spawn) nor expel it from the world. There is yet another being in the waters, (made), not to satisfy our needs, but only to torment us. When we see that we are not capable of exterminating them, we will know our impotence, and we will fall back on our vain pride, and to that alone we will give the victory, who through tiny beings tires us, and subjects us the most large animals; for example, elephants and camels, and lions, and leopards, and panthers, (animals) half of which God fashions and tames, to (serve as) beasts of burden, and the other half for amusement (of man).

12. But others thought differently from Satan, (believing) that God himself made him evil.

Now, if God made him evil, why does the Church cast out demons? If demons have been established as avengers of evils, the Church therefore wrongs those who are admonished by them and opposes the will of God; for (God) made demons for the correction (of man), and he casts them out; but this power to drive them out, (man) does not have it from himself, but from God, (this) is evident. Unless the Lord had first breathed his spirit on the twelve, and given power to the seventy (disciples), they could not cast out the demons; moreover, if (God) himself knew the demons capable of correcting men, he would not take action against them, and he would not order his disciples to cast out (demons), to whom he had ordered to enter into men.

And how could it be (true) that the angels, when they hear the name of God, become joyful, and the demons never; but even more, when they hear (the name of God), they lose their temper. If the repressors of sins were the demons, they would never dispose men to idolatry, nor to different sects of philosophers and heretics, nor to the distribution of spells, nor to the decrees of destiny, etc., nor to fixing the eyes on the stars, (by belief) that they are the cause of prosperity and adversity.

Invention of demons is idolatry; David testifies that all the gods of the pagans are demons. And blessed Paul said: * What relationship has Christ with Belial? And behold, as they say, there is a connection between them; for if, because God has made him evil, (Belial) persecutes (men), we must not call him evil, but vengeful; for evil then would he be, if he did not fulfill the command (of God).

But why not (Satan), but did the angel of God strike the elders of the Egyptians, and many times the Jews in the desert, for if (Satan) was appointed for this, why did he not strike not? But the angel (smote), and in the days of David seventy thousand (men) of the twelve tribes of Israel, and of the camp of Assyria one hundred and seventy-five thousand troops were smitten by the angel of God, and not by demons. Why in the days of Jesus, son of Josedech, did the angel say to the tempter who opposed him: The Lord will punish you, Satan? Why also the Jews are called sons of Satan, because of their transgression of the laws, if he (Satan) remains (faithful) to the order he received, and they (the Jews) have transgressed it? And why should he be called false who righteously abides in order, for from him (Satan) is not wickedness, but from him who made him so; and why will (Satan) be sent into outer darkness?

But, they say, rest is darkness for him. This is not what the legion of demons shouted, but (they shouted) that torments are prepared for him (Satan). * What do we have in common with you, he said, Son of God, that you have come before the time to torment us? And to make his perversity evident, God says: No one can take the instruments of the strong unless he first binds the strong. Now, why would he bind him, if not because he knew that by will he is wicked, and when he wishes, he can become wise?

If, from his birth, God had appointed him to persecute (men), why would he be branded with the name of evil (Satan) who would preserve nature as (as it) was (given) to him? nay more, he would not be worthy of punishment, for having justified his nature; for no one punishes the fire (and says): Why do you burn? nor the waters, (saying): Why are you drowning? And then, as for the (immutable) orders, the questions are resolved in the same direction.

13. By order, they say, will men die, or without orders?

First, we must know what these orders are, and from where the term of these orders through the world extended?

The order linked (or destiny) to the subject of death we find nowhere in the divine books (the Bible); for the master of death and life can shorten his command, and prolong it, as in the time of the flood he said: The days of the life of these men will be a hundred and twenty years; and because of the multitude of iniquities he took away twenty years; and as to Adam, he said: The day you eat of the fruit of this tree, you die; and in his goodness, and because of the filiation and propagation of men in this world, he granted Adam nine hundred and thirty years, so that his beautiful creature would not be totally annihilated; and because of the tears of King Hezekiah, he added fifteen years to his life; and, because of the penitence of the Ninevites, he did not lose their city on the third day, according to the preaching of his prophet.

And not like the Chaldean astrologers, who attribute the causes of births and deaths to the stars as to living (beings); as if, when we are born, from that moment the deaths of each person were inevitably fixed; and, according to this, it was not possible for anyone that the (time of) dying was brought forward or delayed.

But they are confounded by the events of the battles; for in a single day myriads of men are exterminated at different ages, half still children, and half young men, and others in the full age of old age; (victims) whose births were not (arriving) in the same hour, (but whose) deaths took place at the same time.

And then, if stars were (drawn) the causes of births, why in India is no one born white, and in other countries it is not the same color? Has not here only arrived the star which makes white, nor in other countries the star which makes black? And the Indian's teeth, why are they so white?

14. Then they suppose the causes of happiness and misfortune; as if there were sidereal houses, and (that), according to the arrival of the causative stars in these sidereal houses, similar births occurred.

When the lion, they say, is still in his sidereal house, and someone is born, (this man) is to become king. And, when it is the bull and someone is born, this man must arrive strong and well constituted. And when it is the ram, and someone is born, that man is to become rich, and, like the ram, he is thick and hairy. And, when it is the scorpion, and someone is born, that man is likely to become wicked and guilty. And the others (stars) are causes of different things. As if, when Chronos (or Saturn) enters his sidereal house, the king dies, (entrance of Saturn) which took place three times, as they say, under the emperor Theodosius; and the Chaldeans (or astrologers) were assured that the king died, and he (Theodosius) did not die, so that (doomed to) shame would be their lying art.

First, let them say who attracted these earthly names, these carnivorous and herbivorous beings into the heavens, so that they became the causes of the birth of men? for whoever can become the cause of someone's birth, (far) above the one of whom he is the cause, must be in wisdom. Now, by considering (things) with common sense, we will see who is superior, we will see who is above, the man who commands the brute, or the brute who is under the empire of man? And not only is it under his empire, but also it is his food, and of the wild beasts we see half become fugitives, and half in the thick pine forests strengthen themselves, when they only hear the word of man; for the Creator has cast fear and awe of man upon wild beasts and reptiles, and brutes and birds, to better honor (man), whose creature God presents (as a) marvel, that which he created with his own hands, and (on which) he breathed the life-breath, so to speak, from his own mouth. And by this very fact, God shows that he wants to show man more honorable (than other creatures.)

But God is above articulated bodies, this is evident to sincere (men); and, if for him (man) wild beasts and brutes were made, as the experience of things shows, how could it have (happened) that (these beasts) ascended to the heavens, and there became the causes of birth of men, (these beasts) who are as far from vitality as (is) the torch, which by men is composed to serve as light for the house during the night? And objects not having life, how can they become the cause of living beings?

But, if (the stars) were not (beings) living, they say, (the stars) would not be walking, but, since they walk, it is obvious that they are alive.

Now let them hear (this): If everything that moves were alive, then the waters that move would be said to be alive. And fire, because of its movement, would be considered alive. And the air, and the winds, because of their breathing, will be said to be alive. And the plants, the shoots of herbs which, although moving slowly, nevertheless by their growth seem (beings) ambulant. Now, as everything that is itinerant does not have a reflected and reasonable vitality, so also neither the sun, nor the moon, nor the stars, nor the very heavens through which they revolve, have a reflected and reasonable vitality. reasonable. But the heavens and the earth, (like) vessel-receptacles, are established by the Creator (to) contain, enclose in them all that is between them. And the luminous bodies, like torches lit to ward off the darkness from the midst of the great house (of this world). They are obligatory inhabitants for the convenience of all living (beings). They are not themselves, for they do not know whether they are or whether they are not. As also the heavens and the earth, and the woods, and the stones are for those for whom they were (made), and are not themselves theirs; for they do not know whether they are or whether they are not, for the very reason that they are not reflective and reasonable (beings).

Then, as they say: When the lion is in his sidereal house, a king must be born. If it were so, many times many kings would have to be born; for not one (individual) is born when the lion is in his sidereal house, but many.

And, if precisely the lion was the cause of the birth of kings, then the son of the king would not become king, but (it would be) the one whose birth would happen at the entry of the lion into his sidereal house. Now if we see that the king's son becomes king, as David's son Solomon sat on his father's throne, and that man's son (that is, Solomon's) on his throne. And successively the series of kings of Judah was extended until the Maccabees. Likewise also, as for the Assyrians and the Babylonians, the son received from the father by order (of succession) the crown; as also from a certain Sassan, the Sassanids took from father to son, by order of succession, the throne of the Sassanids until today. And the lion was not found in the heavens entered into his sidereal house, that he might carry the throne to another race in the land of the East.

15. It is evident that, as the star is not the cause of the kingdom, so also it is not the cause either of power or of wealth. Especially, since we see the rich becoming poor, and the poor becoming great. Will they also be able to say that: one and the same star can become the cause of greatness and poverty, of power and weakness? for often we see the mighty become weak, and the weak become mighty, and the wicked become wise, and the wise become wicked. And where then is it that they say that: Whatever is written in the orders of destiny, it is not possible to escape, but that he who has been written glorious, is glorious, and he (who has been registered) unhappy is unhappy? And that where the orders (of destiny) are and by whom these orders (have fixed it), so one dies. And it is not possible to escape the established order.

O impotent order, powerless rule, which thieves and bandits can overthrow, when, arising, they throw someone out of his possessions and from the sun (of life); and if, according to a fixed order, things are done, it must not (be permitted) for kings to give orders for death, nor for judges to pursue and put to death the homicide; they who, by imposing the death penalty on (criminals), thus demonstrate that the crimes of the guilty do not happen according to a fixed order, but according to the violence of their wickedness.

Or, when a bandit attacks a country to rob the lord and exterminate the inhabitants, let us not gather troops, let us not form legions upon legions to drive the brigand out of the country; but let him be given (full) right (by saying): If the orders of destiny are to let the country be exterminated by the bandit, why should we turn against these orders? But by gathering troops, by chasing the enemy from the country, we show that it is not according to a fixed order that these depredations are committed, but according to the violence of the brigand who, having come there out of greed, pillages the country, and strips it of its goods and possessions.

16. But we must also know that all the damage that is done by evildoers, God knows in advance.

And if he knows, they say, the damage that must happen (or fall) on men, why does he not prevent it?

How much harm God averts from men; this is not obvious to all, but to him alone who distributes (to all) his providence according to the needs of each. He sometimes shortens the damage (caused by) evildoers, lest it thus appear that he cannot prevent this damage. Then he also allows the evildoer to satisfy his (brutal) wills on his companion, lest (him God) appear to lead reasonable (beings) by necessity, but (also), so that by the works of each one appear everyone's ways of being.

And in advance (God) knows everything, and this foreknowledge is not the cause of evils; for when someone sees his companion going through precipices, and says that (this man) will be thrown down, (this someone) was not the cause of the fall of his companion; nor, when anyone sees his companion going through places infested with thieves, and says that this man will find his ruin there, this (anyone will not be the cause of the damage; nor, when anyone sees the son of a noble person will come to the dissipation, and will say that this (young man) will lose the paternal goods, this someone will not be the cause of the dissipation of these goods; likewise also, the foreknowledge of God is not the cause goods or evils.

God knows everything in advance; but there are (things) that he wants, there are things that he does not want. He wanted to produce the flood, and his will was not that man and the brute in general should be exterminated, but the perversity of the infamous disorders of the human race led him to the point of doing what he did not want; as he himself swears by his prophet, (saying): * I do not want the death of the sinner, but his return (to good) and his life.

(God) wanted Adam not to sin; and, as he knew in advance his transgression, he ordered him in advance not to eat of the fruit of the tree; and as (Adam) did not obey the order, he was justly punished. In advance, (God) knew with regard to Job that he would be virtuous; and, concerning Esau, that he would get lost in the disorders. And for this reason, even before they were born, he said: I have loved Jacob, and I have hated Esau. And in advance, considering the zeal of Josiah, king of Judah, he warned in advance through his prophet that from them there must arise a king who will destroy the idolatry of the children of Israel. And in advance, having made known the excellence of the Persian Cyrus, he announces in advance that he must deliver his people from captivity: it is obvious that knowing in advance (the future) is the height of the marvelous essence of God.

17. Wanting good and not evil was the beneficence of his philanthropic nature. Considering in advance Pharaoh's obstinacy, God said: I will harden Pharaoh's heart.

And if he hardened him, they say, why did he strike him and the land of Egypt with harsh blows?

But the apostle enters into justification of his master (by saying) that * not (God) hardened Pharaoh, but he hardened himself. And this saying of God: I have hardened, is like (what says) someone, when he has glorified his companion or his servant, and the latter becomes proud, will despise the one who raised him: (the benefactor) will say: * Why should I blame him? I myself have done this insult to myself, because I brought to honor an unworthy man;

in the same way, we must understand regarding God: I was by my indulgence the cause of his hardness, because I did not first exterminate his firstborn.

But (God) wanted, says the apostle, to show his anger and manifest his power, which he extended with much longsuffering on vessels prepared for perdition. From which it is evident that the longsuffering of God was the cause of the hardening of Pharaoh's heart, by the very fact that God did not first launch the last blows on him.

But, as (God) had not petrified the heart of Pharaoh, by this we must understand that sometimes (Pharaoh) consented to let the people (of God) go, and sometimes did not consent. They themselves became vessels prepared for perdition, and not God (made them thus, God) of whom the apostle says that: He wants all men to live and come to the knowledge of the truth. And were they not then they (of the number) of all men?

And not, as (our) opposing party says, that (man acts) not according to his will, nor even according to his walk, but according to the mercy of God; for on whom he wishes (to have pity), he has pity, and on whom (he wishes to punish), he punishes. Also, confusing the side of our adversaries, the apostle says: Who are you, O you, O man, who demands an answer from God? If it were like this here, who would you be who would demand accountability from God? Did the clay say to the potter: why have you made me thus? But it is not so. (The apostle) himself, in the same epistle, says it: To the obedience of whomever you wish, you devote your persons, (to the obedience) of justice or to the obedience of sin. And, writing to Timothy, (the apostle) said: If anyone purifies himself, he has become a vessel usefully prepared for the work of his Lord; and the prophet said: If you please to listen to me, you will eat the goodness of the earth.

From all this and many other things it is evident that (God) does not arrange vessels of wrath for perdition, nor vessels of mercy for glory, but that (men) themselves arrange for perdition or for glory; and, as there is no partiality on the part of God, (the apostle) says: Would he be God only of the Jews, and not also

REFUTATIONS

of the pagans? Yes, (he is also God) of the pagans; for it is the same God who justifies circumcision by faith, and uncircumcision by the same faith. Then (he also says * about us) whom he called not only from among the Jews, but also from among the Gentiles. And elsewhere (he says): He is one Lord, one faith, one baptism, one God over all and for all and in everything.

Then, having previously threatened his people with captivity, God said with an oath: I have spoken, now I will do (what I have spoken), and I will not turn back (my words). Not that this was his will, but their impiety led him to what he did not want. And, if in the same obstinacy, after these threats, (the Jews) did not persevere, (God) would not deliver them into the hands of their enemies. He preferred to evade his word than to deliver them into the hands of infidels; as, considering the penitence of the Ninevites, he did not destroy their city.

Then (God), in advance, considering Jeremiah: When you were not yet traced (in embryo) in the womb (of your mother), I knew you, he said, in order to show that in advance he knew what it should be; and (God) inscribed him among the saints by the very fact that he said: When you were not yet out of the womb (of your mother), I sanctified you and gave you (for) a prophet to the nations.

Likewise also as to Samuel, and to John, and to Paul; as he himself (the apostle) says: He chose me from my mother's womb to proclaim the Gospel of his Son through me; and all the saints whom, as the apostle says, (God) knew in advance, he marked in advance to be conformed to the image of his Son. And then: He chooses us before the world even existed.

And God is (always) willing what is good; (this is what) our Lord teaches saying that: This is the will of my Father who is in heaven, that everyone who sees the Son, and believes in him, shall receive life in eternity. And then (he says) that: This is my food, that I do the will of my Father; and it is the will of my Father that as many as my Father has given me, I should not let them be lost from him, but should raise them up at the last day.

Therefore (God) wills that all who believe in his Son should not be lost but should be raised to life on the day of resurrection; and the work of resurrection, after many generations, must take place. But God had these good wills from the beginning and still has them. These are not wills that come into him, but natural wills, according to his unspeakable goodness; and, as before we said, his will always delights in good, and he wants his rational creatures to desire good, and to do works of justice.

But, as he knows that half (of men) walk according to his will, and half do not walk (in the same way), because of this, the virtue of some, to excite others to zeal for good, he the announcement from the womb (of their mother); in the same way also he announces the unworthiness of others; not that God will create one virtuous from the womb, and the other unworthy; and, if this were so, what need would there be to praise (the virtuous man), and to denounce the one who is not? Moreover, vice should not be indicted because God would have created it in this way from the mother's womb.

Therefore, it is obvious that this saying of God: I loved Jacob and I hated Esau, is knowing in advance that this one (Jacob) would be lovable by his morals, and this one (Esau) hateful; and as, (in fact), by his morals Esau was hateful, the apostle says that: No one (is) a fornicator and impure like Esau; and let no one, (like a) root of bitterness arising, oppress others; and (God) thus manifested that according to his own will such was Esau, and not by (the effect of) the creation of God. As also elsewhere (the apostle) says that: God made man upright (and just), and (man) meditated thoughts of wickedness. And (God) said by his prophet: I have planted you a delicious vine, and how have you become bitter for me, an uncultivated vine?

18. From which it is evident that God makes the creation of all beautiful, and that to turn to good and evil he has made their independence free, so that the side he wishes (each) can turn, and according to his works receive similar remuneration. Let (man) not behave like the brute, for whom no act is good (and for whom there is) no hope of remuneration, for the very fact that he is the brute, and that he does not know how to choose and distinguish good from evil through thought, but according to his natural instincts. By these

reminiscences alone, (the brute) is driven to (what is) useful to him and protects himself from (what is) harmful.

For brutes, there are aptitudes by which their species must be prepared for certain things; as (the species) of the horse by its hoof (is fit) to run, that of the ox in winter to rest in the stable, and at the approach of spring to turn towards the door; that of the swallow before the autumn (is prepared) to go to warm places in winter quarters. (The species) of the crane (is able) to sense considerable cold and to leave early for warm places. (The species) of the stork (has the instinct) early to circulate in flocks. (The species) of pigeons (is disposed) to fly in compact flocks. (The species) of crows, to go quickly from cold countries to hot countries. (The species) of vultures is suited to spying on carrion from afar.

And (so) of all other brutes and birds; as (the species) of ants (is suited) to store its food, and to cut the grain in two, so that it does not germinate, and in hot weather to draw these grains from the hole and to dry them. (The species) of bees (is capable) of blocking the doors of hives with wax before the cold. (The species) of the bear (is able) to enter its den before winter. (The species) of the deer (is suitable) to come early from the mountains to the plain. (The species) of deer (is specific) to knowing precisely the time of mating. (The species) of wild donkeys with vindictive instinct, (is suitable) to cut donkeys at a young age. And all these instincts are natural in brutes and not reflexed; they were, by their creator, implanted in them to dispose them to (what is) useful to them, and to divert them from (all things) harmful.

19. And not only in brutes are these instincts natural, but also in men, who are endowed with speech and wisdom; as when the eye is moving, it is by the effect of a natural warning to see some new person, a (certain) sign, say those who often pay attention to this. When in the loins or other limb the flesh is agitated, it is a sign of a man riding a horse, or dressed in magnificent clothes, or meeting a friend, or receiving a caning. Likewise also, when the foot stings or the hand, the first (case), they say, is a sign of travel or rain, and the other (case is a sign) of taking from someone or giving something. Likewise, sneezing and biting the tongue, fluttering of the ears, tingling of the throat, this does not happen by the

REFUTATIONS

act of some genius, but by a natural influence that the creator has implanted in the members, so that, when the man will be distracted from meditative attention, he will be surrounded by a natural influence.

Yawning and lying down, as some have thought, does not come from the devil, but from the softness and nonchalance of the body; hence (it follows that) frequent yawning and lying down come, say skilful doctors, from the mass of humors, which experience demonstrates; for when someone yawns often, a shiver runs through his bones, a tremor runs through his limbs.

Sneezing does not come from an angel, but from the cold, or from some other natural influence. Moreover, sighing sometimes takes place through reminiscence, and sometimes even without remembering someone. And, as these are natural influences, and not (coming from) demons, it is evident that even in brutes the same natures are found. To sigh, when this takes place without remembering anyone, or something good, or needs, is a natural warning, to concentrate man under the fear of his creator, and to know the weakness of his nature. And, when it happens (to sigh) out of memory, it is out of attachment to a friend, or for having suffered some indignity, some damage: as when someone, in waking life, abandons himself to inertia, he is, through (the effect of) nocturnal dreams, concentrated under (the influence of) fear.

20. And different dreams are the causes. There are things that a man will have uttered in the evening; of these same things, when the body rests and sleeps, the mind is occupied. There are also things which man has not thought at all, and which he sees in dreams. And there are two causes for this:

Or see something determined, as in a mirror, for example, (effect produced) by the influence of God's graces to exhort man to good, and not by the reality of something obviously present; as to Joseph and Daniel, visions of great things appeared.

(It is also) some (effect produced) by the enemy (of men); for it is incorporeal, as the breath of man (is) incorporeal; and, taking different forms, he traces

REFUTATIONS

them before us, sometimes (forms) of women, to excite us to concupiscence, and sometimes forms of frightful animals and reptiles to frighten (us); as Job said: * With dreams you terrify me. And many times, appearing in the form of women, (the demon) deceives men in dreams. It also sometimes happens that, returning in the form of men, he causes women to fail. It is not that he has male and female members, but, stirring the vessel of concupiscence, he causes (the sign of) virility to spread; not (that), when he has entered into an individual, and has engaged in male or female discourses (of sensuality), we must believe that there is a male or female state in him. Nor, when he shows that he fears the stick or the sword, should we believe that; because for him, the rod is the reprimand of God and the graces of the saints which they receive from the Holy Spirit. Or else, in a state of wakefulness or in the rest of sweet sleep, he shows that he fears the staff and the sword, so that by stopping men at this idea, he will make them relax the task of asking God for help. (This is what the Lord himself indicated by saying: This species (of demons) only leaves through fasting and prayer.

No, not all error, not all delirium of men is (produced) by the demon; but there are (these disorders) which come from the bile, there are those from the humours, there are those from the exhaustion of the spinal cord, there are those from the disturbed stomach, there are those from the stomach hardened, to the point of foaming and convulsing the eyes.

21. But, as a result of the exhaustion of the spinal cord, man falls (deprived) of his intelligence, speaks with the walls, fights against the winds; hence (it follows that) doctors maintain that there is no demon that enters into man, but these are pains; and, we (they say), with remedies we can cure them.

But (we) do not say that; for true for us is the word of the Gospel (which says) that: Many demons, when they saw Jesus, cried out and came out of men. * And he (Jesus) punished them and did not give them permission to speak. (Such is this conclusive passage) with others of the same kind. And those who are called lunatics are so called, not because the moon (is) harmful to them, but it is an order of demons who manifest themselves according to (the phases of) the moon.

REFUTATIONS

Satan can only tempt as much as he is commanded, this is evident from the temptations of Job; for, if he had not first received the order from God, he would not have dared to attempt (Job); and also, according to * the herd of swine into which the demons could not enter, unless they had taken the command of the Lord.

22. But there are some who say that Satan does not tempt man at all.

But they are confounded by the apostle, who says that: Many times I wanted to come to you, and Satan prevented me. And he says again: There is no fight for us with the body and with the blood, but rather against the powers, and against the dominations, and against the conquerors of this world of darkness. And (God) says in the Gospel that: Satan had put into the heart of Judas Iscariot the thought of delivering (Jesus), and then that Satan entered through a crack; then again: * Satan asked to sift you like wheat.

(God) gives Satan power to tempt as much as man can bear (temptation); as the blessed apostle says that: God is sincere, he will not throw you into temptation more than (is great) your power (of resistance); but he will make you (find) with the temptation the means to escape from it, so that you can endure it. And our Lord teaches in his prayer to say: Lead us not into temptation but deliver us from evil. To show that through prayers we can escape the temptations of evil.

23. If it is so, they say, to tempt God has established (Satan). But we have shown above, by numerous testimonies from the Holy Books, that (it is) not to torment and to tempt (men) that God did it. But through him (Satan), who hastened into wickedness, God does a good work. Although the wicked come not with this intention to tempt; but he thinks he has won and finds himself defeated. God lets him according to his bad will tempt the virtuous (men), and (these), entering into the temptations (of Satan), as in the crucible, are refined and extracted like pure gold coming out of the furnaces.

Now, if God had made Satan minister of evils, in the days of Ahab, the imposter spirit would not have (come) to the mouth of the false prophets. But he (Satan) had to perform this service. And why should not the spirit, which does not confess the Lord Jesus, be (emanated) from God, he (spirit) which does not deceive the service of God? And why should those who do not believe in the Lord Jesus be called sons of evil, if (evil or Satan) by the word of God is a tempter? and, if the Jews are the children of evil, the executor of God's will, why is Abraham not so named? and why is false and homicidal called evil, if it stands in truth and not in falsity?

We will write again (this): If the Jew of himself speaks falsely, why is he (Satan) called father of the Jew, he (Satan) who does not distort his nature, but as he was (made), thus speak? And why will the apostle say that: Satan must obey our Savior unto death, and fall from his power and his dominion, he (Satan) who wanted by himself to make himself God? And why will (Satan) be chained and delivered to torment? Is it not that by his will he sought to take from men the worship (due) to God, and attract them to idolatry, and, by enchantments, spells and astrology, he turns men away from the truth of God? ?

And (Satan) is called an enemy (of man) because he sows tares among the wheat. From which it is evident that not by nature he is enemy (of man), but by will. And, if by nature it was given to him not to know God the father, how could he know his Son and cry: * You are the son of God? And then, touching the apostles, (how could he) say that: * These men are the servants of the most high God?

And from all this it is evident that (Satan) is not evil by nature, but by will. Neither wicked nor persecutor has made God, but by his willfully evil ways, (Satan) makes the righteous virtuous. And from him there is no grace in this.

24. And the luminous (bodies), as we said previously, are not living beings, and causes of good or evil, but only the service for which they were intended, they fulfill; as Moses said that: * God made the great luminous bodies and placed them in the firmament of the heavens to give their light to the earth. From which it is evident that, to give their light, only they were made, and also to (serve as) a sign to times and days, to months and years, not as living beings, but

as (bodies) luminous to give light to (objects) which are under the heavens, and to show certain signs of the knowledge of God, of the rains and of the changes of the airs: as our Lord says: * When you see in the morning the heavens purple, you say the rain will come, and it will come. * And when the south wind blows, you say that there will be great heat, and it does.

For, at sunrise, the air having taken the moisture from the waters, throws them around the rays of the sun, and, as the air is not yet thickened, and become cloudy; by stopping its brightness somewhat, it only reddens the sun and does not obscure it. Hence it seems that it is a sign of rain.

Likewise, the moon, hampered by the humidity in the air, strives to remove this humidity. From which (it follows that) this humidity, approaching and not reaching (the moon), kept enclosed, thickens around it; that by which the sign of rain is made evident; and not only for the moon, but also for a torch, which is a much smaller light, this is noticeable.

25. And the heavens do not rotate, whatever the wise pagans say, that sometimes by rotating they hide the luminous bodies, and sometimes they reveal them; and, if they turned all day, how would they bring the sun every day to the same east, and the moon, in barely the (same) month, to the same places? There are still other stars which, in barely a year, arrive once at the same places. (There) are some (who), as they say, in twelve years (arrive) at the same place; (there) is (who) in a year and a half, (there) is (who) in thirty years.

But, in the experience of things, the opposite is evident; for the stars which are in the heavens until dawn are there until evening. If the heavens turned, in the same paths where we see them at dawn, they would no longer be found in the evening. But, as in the same paths they walk, as also we see the moon and the stars in the same paths, it is evident that they (the stars) walk, and that the heavens remain immobile, sedentary, like also the books themselves given by God (the Bible) call firmament the heavens, and that which is firmament is not movable.

REFUTATIONS

But, of other books taking pretext, they say: In these books it is written that God placed the stars in the firmament of the heavens: from which it is evident that they are nailed there, and not moving.

But if it were so, when God says of Adam that he has placed him in the paradise of delights, they will then believe him to be nailed there, and not walking? Now, if the movement of Adam, the divine books call it (by this word) he put, it is obvious that the movement of luminous bodies, the (divine) books name it (by this word) he has put. Especially since in many places we find luminous (bodies) walking; as when Joshua, son of Nun, said that: The sun stood over the valley of Gibeon, and the moon over the plain of Aialon. And he does not say that the heavens stopped in their progress, but (the bodies) luminous; from which it is evident that the heavens were stationary, and the luminous (bodies) moved. And under Hezekiah it is said: The light shall shift back ten degrees from the palace of Ahaz. By this it appears that the sun returned back, and not the heavens. And in Ecclesiastes it is written that the sun rises and the sun sets, and it expands in its place. * The sun being up, walks towards the south and stretches towards the north. To show that in the evening he goes south to the west, and at daybreak returns to the north to the east by the base of the mountains, as the wise say, and not by sea, as they say, them, and not underground; for under the earth there is nothing, as Job says: * (God) has spread the earth over nothing. And in Syria it is said that (God) placed the earth on nothing. Now, for something, it is not possible to walk on nothing, or for continental nature (that is to say dry) to be in the humidity of waters.

But, they say, we see with our eyes that from the sea comes (the sun).

And they do not know that, because somewhere the continent does not appear from the sea, therefore it appears that it comes out of the sea: as when someone is near the west, and a mountain is on the east side, it seems to him that the sun comes out of the mountain; and in all places, wherever someone is, it seems to him that near that place the sun comes out. Likewise also for those who stand near the sea, as it is not possible to make the eye open on the continent, it seems that from the sea comes (the sun), which from the sea does not come out, but from the ends of the heavens; as David, instructed by the Holy Spirit, says that:

* From the end of the heavens is the going out of the sun, and its rest (or setting) when (it arrives) at the same end.

But the sun, they say, throws into the world a strong dew, from which it is evident that it comes from the sea.

And they do not know that the air, which, at night, swells with the humidity of the waters, the heat of the sun's rays having arrived, shakes and disperses this humidity; hence it happens that not only here, but all over the earth, at sunrise the dew falls.

And, if the heavens rotated, how, touching Chronos and the other causative stars, will they say that they enter their sidereal residences, (those stars) whose entry would therefore be by walking and not without walking?

26. But the earth also, they say, stands in space, and they give this example: A bladder, when you want to blow it, throws in a grain of millet; and the wind, which is an obstacle in the bladder, takes the grain of millet and holds it in space, neither letting it come up above nor rush down below; in the same way, they say, the air, which is in the middle of the globe of the heavens, remains enclosed there, and keeps the world in a happy medium, neither above it allows it to rise, nor below bow down.

First by their own words they are confounded; for they say that what is light upwards goes forward, and what is heavy downwards; as also the experience of things demonstrates: for the smoke and the vapor of the earth, and the flame of the fire, as they are (things) light, towards the upper part advance; and stone, and iron, and wood, and even other things of the same kind, as much as they are drawn upwards, as much as they are drawn downwards they descend; and, if the slightest weight, the air cannot support it above, how much more for the immense weight of the earth, it is not possible for the air to support it elevated, but (this is possible) to the word of God who established the earth on nothing.

REFUTATIONS

And (he) who doubts how such a weight can stand on nothing, seeing the firmament of the heavens which stands on nothing, let him consent (to believe) that he who, by his word, established the heavens on nothing, also holds by its order both (the heavens and the earth) immobile and stationary; according to what he himself said: * And (the heavens and the earth) were; he commanded, and they were established, and he set them there for ever and ever. * He has imposed his order, and (his order) will not pass away.

And they say other things. If the earth stands on nothing, how does David say that (God) * established the earth on the waters? * And then, that on the sea he laid the foundations of (the earth), and on the rivers prepared it.

He who learned this from David will learn something else from Job and Isaiah; for they say (the established earth) about nothing, and David (says) * about the waters. Now, not contrary to each other are the (holy) books; but what one (of these books) omitted, another completes it, (inspired) by the same (holy) Spirit, as we see that what Moses did not say, the other prophets completed it (inspired) by the same Spirit. Moses said: * God created man from the ground of the earth, and then breathed the divine breath. Now, (this word) blowing is still in the realm of opinion: (knowing) whether blowing would be a creature here, or not. Now the prophet Zechariah comes, moved by the same (holy) Spirit, and he shows the creature of this breath; he says: (God) * who establishes the breath of man in him; and Isaiah said: Everything (that which is) breathes, (it is I) who have made it.

Likewise also, neither fire, nor water, nor air, nor lightning, nor thunder, nor darkness speaks to Moses, (things) which must be understood to have come out of the two great vessels, the heavens and earth; (by what is said) that: * Whatever is between them (heaven and earth), all this must have been done with; according to what (is said) that * God made heaven and earth and all that is in them.

27. But lest, worthy of the honors of an independent constitution, appear (to the) ignorant (the things) whose creation is not recorded by Moses, to cut off

REFUTATIONS

the pretexts of the arguers, (behold), by the other prophets, the same Holy Spirit presents the creation of these (things).

First David (confirms the fact), by this (even) that all imaginable powers, and all creatures, he calls them to the glorification of the Creator, when he says: * Bless him, heaven and earth, angels and powers, and fire, and winds, and storms, which do (the will of) his word; and, that which enters into office, and performs a service, it is evident that they are creatures.

And the snow, and the ice, and the hail, and the storms, if from another creator they had (come out), the (holy) Spirit would not call them to the glorification (of God), but, as (foreign things), he would put them aside; but we see that not only these things, but also dragons, and wild beasts, and darkness, and lightning, which they suppose (emanate) from evil, to the same glorification the same (holy) Spirit calling them , and, by David, and by the three children in the furnace, presents (to us) to show that for him, by whom they were made, (all these things) are called justly to his glorification.

And not, as Marcion falsely says, that it is the duty of the just creatures to offer worship to the stranger, because of his beneficence. His immortality, in due course, we will refute.

28. And now, although from this it is evident that that which is called to the glorification of the Creator is his creature; but of each of these things it is necessary, according to the (holy) books, to show (the state) of creature.

First (creature) of angels, as David says, that: (God) made the angels his spirits, and his minister the flame of fire; then creatures of fire and other things one after the other. He made his lightning in the rain. Not that the lightning comes from nowhere (emanates), except from the nature of fire; and of the darkness he said: Thou didst set the darkness, and there was night. And of the thunder and the wind together, Moses says that: to him who establishes the thunder, and establishes the wind, Lord Almighty is his name. And so, what one prophet omitted, through another (prophet) the Holy Spirit completes it.

REFUTATIONS

Now if David says that * on the waters is the earth, by Job and Isaiah (it is said) that on nothing it stands. We should not be surprised (at this difference in language), nor should we believe the prophecies that are contrary to each other; for this is true, and this is constant. And take an example of the body, on which is the skin and the flesh, and between (are) the veins and the vessels of the blood, and underneath again (there is) also skin and flesh; and the body is therefore above the veins of the blood, and below the veins. According to this example, the earth is on the waters; for in its midst it has waters, and beneath it waters. And on nothing it is established stationary, and has contained within itself the fluid nature of the waters; and of these two prophecies there is only one and the same inspection, and there is no allegory; for it (is) not one spirit, then another (who) gave this prophecy, but it is the same and only spirit which found it good to make one a historian of certain things, and the others, historians (facts) left out by him.

Now, that the heavens do not rotate, that everything that was not and was is creature, and not constituted of itself, the examples of the first natures, the testimonies of the holy books were sufficient to convince the minds of this truth exercised; but, as they persist (them) in the same ineptitude, regarding everything (as) living and breathing, we will not neglect, according to our power, to respond also to this (absurdity).

BOOK THREE
REFUTATION OF THE RELIGION OF THE SAGES OF GREECE

1. The moon, they say, thirty days earlier than the sun, passing through all the sidereal houses, that is to say through all the heavens, arrives at the same place (from where it left); and the sun in a year, and the heavens (in) a day and a night, carried around themselves, turn (and return) to the same place. And only seven stars are moving, and all the others are nailed to the heavens; and the stars which (are) itinerant are the sun and the moon, and five more stars, (it is) not from east to west that they walk, but from west to east.

And they give an example which is not similar: they (say) that, when a wheel turns, and an ant, (placed) in an earthen vessel, moves from east to west, because of the rapid evolution of the wheel towards the west, it seems that the ant goes from east to west; not that (really) it goes from east to west, but (well) from west to east. And the wheel, by its rapid evolution, makes (the thing) appear thus.

And the heavens, they say, as much as they are above, as they are below, as much on every side, around the earth; and the water envelops the earth, and the air (envelops) the water and the earth; and fire (envelops) and air, and water, and earth; and the moon does not have its particular light, but from the sun comes its light. And from there, it is obvious, they say, that whatever side the sun is, from that side begins to be born for it (moon) the light, and, according to the distance from the sun, comes to it in a little (from quantity) the light, and, according to the approach little by little (of the sun), the light abounds; and, when (the sun) comes close to the moon, it fills it (with light); and, when (the moon) passes the sun, its light begins to diminish a little; and as the moon moves away, so does the light, until it disappears completely; and when another time this happens, then there is no light for the moon because of the distance; and as the moon approaches (the sun), the light gradually increases for it.

And the moon, they say, is lower than the sun and all the stars, and, as it is below, when the balance opposite the sun arrives, then the sun is obscured. And causes the changes (or mutations) of the four natures of elements, they (make) the stars, and suppose them to be living beings. All this they say in blasphemy, in order to pass off the heavens and the stars as living beings, and even as gods.

2. Justly, as the blessed apostle says, that: * By the wisdom of God the world did not know God. And what wonder is there that the heavens, because of their immeasurable grandeur, and the luminous bodies, because of their immense brilliance, they believed them to be gods, when in the wood, and in the stone, and in wild beasts and animals they sought gods? (These are people) whom the very character of their nature condemns, by the very fact that they are in search of the creator, in search of God, and, falling (in error) outside the only truth (God), they came up against many (gods), and nowhere was there stability and stability for them; for to seek God was worthy of praise, and to introduce not one only, but many, is unspeakable impiety.

3. And above all the wise men of Greece are blamed; for when they came to wisdom, they did not know the creator of wisdom; for they also admit something (thing), existing of itself, cause of everything, (cause) not proceeding from anyone, but existing of itself, first (principle) found. Secondly, they admit God, and creator of intelligence, and thirdly breath, which they call soul of everything.

By supposing these two (last beings) emanated from a single cause, they showed that they were approaching the doors of the science of truth; and by making other perceptible and apparent gods proceed from these beings by birth, and to infinity, they themselves closed the doors to the knowledge of faith; because, like the sun and its rays, they suppose God, and even perceptible, apparent gods, and the world entirely co-eternal with him (God); and in everything, his spirit as the breath of everything, and in the heavens, and in the luminous bodies, and in the fire, and in the air, and in the waters, and in the earth, even in the stones, and the woods, and the trees, and the roots even of the grass. And through this vitality, they say, all creatures depend on its nature, as the rays of

REFUTATIONS

the sun depend on the wheel itself, (that is) on the disk (of the sun). He (God) is one and many, many and one, as the sun is one and many, for it is one wheel or disk, and many spokes. And this, they do not all say it like this, but there are several religions of philosophers.

4. The Pythagoreans and Peripatetics say (that there is) unity (of God), and providence, and (command) not to sacrifice to the gods. Pythagoras established (as a principle of) religion not to eat the flesh of beings having breath, and to abstain from wine; all that is of the moon and above (the moon) to be deemed immortal, and all that is below mortal; (to admit) the permutation of breaths or souls from body to body, up to brutes and (other) animals. And (Pythagoras) established the religion of silence, and then he called himself God.

But the Platonists (admit) God, and ὕλη, and idea; the first (of these last two things) is matter, the second the property of each individual. (They also admit) the creature world, and destructible, and the uncreated breath, and immortal, and divine, the three parts of which are the reasonable, the angry, the concupiscible, (order to) regard women (as common property or) of all; and (forbids) any man to have (his own) a private wife; but (he wants) the one that men will want, (and the one that) women will agree, to be with each other. (He admits) the transmutation of souls into different bodies, up to animals and reptiles. At the same time, he established several gods from one (God).

But the Stoics admitted a body everywhere and looked upon the apparent world as God. But some of the essence of fire believe that it holds its nature. They decided that God is intelligence, as if the breath of everything was the element of the heavens and the earth. (For) body they gave him all that is, and for eyes (bodies) luminous; they made the bodies of all perishable, and the souls transmutable from body to body.

Now, the Epicureans say: inseparable and indivisible were the bodies first, and from there everything was constituted. And as the supreme end of good, they established concupiscence. And there is no God, no providence that governs everything. This is the religion of the philosophers (Epicureans).

REFUTATIONS

5. But the beginning of paganism, even in the days of Saruch, took place; because an excellent man, having come into the world, died (immediately) to (preserve the) memory of his merit, we drew (the features of) his image in painting; and thereby educated, the ignorant little by little took (this image as an object of) worship; and, what concerns the idols, the sculptures, (took place) under Thara, father of Abraham. Each, with his art, sculpted the same (idol); the blacksmith by forging, the carpenter by carpentry, the silversmith, and the bronze worker, and the stonemason, and the potter, each by means of his art. And from there, thus arranged, came to the Egyptians and the Babylonians, and the Phoenicians, and the Phrygians the work of sculpture and its mysteries; then to the Hellenes, who are the Greeks, under Cecrops; and even later this state of things increased under Chronos, and Rhea, and Jupiter, and Apollo, and many others, whom one after the other they called gods.

And Hellenes are called the Greeks (from the name) of a certain person whose name was Hellenus in the land of the Hellades. But others say that (this name comes) from the olive tree which grew of itself in Athens, because olive tree in Greek is called ελαία.

But the (Greeks or) Ionians (take their name) from Javan who was one of the directors of the construction of the tower; therefore, they are all called Merob, because of the confusion of languages; because division in Greek is called μερισμὸς.

The first religions were called barbarian and Scythian, and pagan, until the worship of the true God of Abraham came, (which) ruined these religions.

And the Judaism (is so called) of Judah, the fourth son of Jacob; from him came the kingdom, and the whole nation took his name, the Jewish name.

And, at the end of Judaism, the name Christianity came from Christ, who (Christianity) was first called thus by the disciples in Antioch.

REFUTATIONS

6. Therefore, the philosophers, in seeking God according to the natural law which is implanted in the intellect, as we said before, are worthy of praise. But to fall into (the error which admits) several gods, to suppose the world co-eternal with God, is enormous impiety. And to these people the apostolic word fits, which says: * They knew God, and they did not glorify him as God.

For the glorification of God was that the honor of the creator was separated from his creatures. By which also the creatures, each by their movements, and their changes, speak (very loudly) of the creator. Now, if the stars, according to their absurdities, were gods, and the heavens, and the sun, and the moon, which are without speech, and without sound, what would then be the cause, more than the objects having cause? And above all, when the intelligence and the breath (of this cause), if we can say the breath of God, they put them in all animate and inanimate creatures naturally (and proceeding) from the essence of him (God). What is unspeakably impiety is to regard the vitality of the essence of God as (that of) animate and inanimate beings in general; and not rather (to regard as) creature vitality in angels, in demons, and in men, who are (beings) reasonable and intelligent; and in other animate (beings) a natural vitality mixed and aggregated from the four matters, which, when (these beings) break (are also broken), and the vitality in these four matters dissolves.

They are the spirits of angels and demons, and the breath of men. Now, with their own words will they not blush those who say the breath (or soul) uncreated, immortal and divine (emanating) from the nature of God himself, and then they admit torments, penalties for prevaricant souls; which is the last blasphemy, if the essence of God was divided into parts, and was tortured in many (these parts or) breaths; and then again that a part (of God) tormented a (another) part of his nature; that one part was (dedicated) to glory, another to contempt, and one part to delights, another portion to hell.

And then they say: If there were not some vitality in everything, how could it be (true) that everything moves? And the seeds and plants thrown into the ground grow. And in the families of men and brutes the fallen seeds come to generation and propagation. This is what we do not deny, because of our experience of things, which makes these facts evident.

REFUTATIONS

But this is the question: (to know) that this vitality is not the vitality of the essence of God, but creature-vitality, different in rational and intelligent beings, and different in brutes, and in (beings) having breath, different again in natural (substances), like the seeds which fall into the females of men, and of brutes. Those of men are much more honorable. In (man) there is natural vitality, according to the body, and reasonable and marvelous vitality, according to the breath (or soul); for the body is composed of the four matters, and the soul (does not emanate) from these four aggregated matters, but from a simple and subtle nature. (The soul) of other brutes is not similar, but (it emanates) from a natural and instinctive nature. (The soul) of the seeds (is) not yet the same, but (it proceeds) from natural and inanimate influences.

7. Likewise also in luminous (bodies) the animation is not reasonable, but natural and influenced movements. Hence some have supposed propelling angels. But we will follow in the footsteps of the holy books, which speak of rains, which * God had not yet caused to rain in torrents on the earth. And not, as some have ridiculously said, that Satan had power to move and change the air, according to what the Apostle says: * According to the prince of the power of this air; he calls him prince of this air, because of his fall from heaven, and his wandering in the air. And hence it is evident what (the Apostle) says, * prince of this dark air, to show that light (Satan) has been cast into darkness, and that he does not change the air sometimes into rain, sometimes snow, sometimes hail.

But this is the work of God, and not of Satan, will say David (inspired) closely by the Holy Spirit, (when he says) that: He (God) * draws the clouds from the extremity of the earth, and he made lightning in the rains, * and he draws the winds from his stores, * and then he puts snow like wool, and mist like the dust of barns, and he throws out the frost like crumbs, etc. And a prophet said: * Let (God) call water from the sea and pour it out on the face of the earth. And Job said that: * Who begat the drops of rain, and out of whose womb comes the frost, who begat the mist in the heavens, which descendeth like water falling drop by drop? to say that this is my work, and not (the work) of anyone else.

Likewise, moving luminous bodies is the work of his word, and not of anyone else. And not only are seven stars moving, (while) the others would be without walking, but all are moving; half slow walking, half fast walking; and they are not nailed to the heavens, as it was said before that, sometimes like a wheel, they turn, and sometimes show themselves, and sometimes hide themselves. And, what is even more worthy of ridicule, (is) that the sun moves from west to east. And why do they not call the west east, and the east west?

But not at all, they say, the sun does not enter (or set) anywhere. It does not enter anywhere, this is obvious, since the night (it is) from its light projected into the vase (or globe) of the moon, that the light rises; for he (the sun) goes away, moves away, and is found in other regions.

And if you say that the sun is in the heavens, the night, the darkness which occurs, from where would it be (produced)?

They say: Through the very shadow of the earth comes darkness.

But (then) the darkness which occurs above in the heavens, from where would it be produced? Is it not evident then that the (sun) is hidden somewhere at night, as can be seen by its setting; for, as from top to bottom it descends, and then, as it ascends, as from bottom to top it rises.

In vain their emphatic speeches! for as great is the house of heaven as that of the earth; for the divine books say the heavens are a cubit, and the earth a palm, and we do not find the cubit greater than the palm.

8. Then, (say) that the moon does not have its own light, first of all their assertion is false if, in its growth in every point, the matter which comes from it grows, and that in its fullness (this matter) completes itself, and in its failure lacks.

As the experience of things shows in all carnal (beings), and in the trees and in the plants, (is) humidity, and in Europe there are certain points of seas whose waters, according to the growth of the moon, increase, and, according to its fullness overflow, and according to its waning diminish. And these (people) are so impudent that they want to capture the eyes of all men, who at night, at sunset, see the light of the moon more resplendent.

How much faster than the sun, would they say the non-existent moon of itself? for, they say, it completes its course in thirty days, and the sun in a year. The experience of things confuses them, as does the divine book which says that: He made two great luminous (bodies), and placed them in the firmament of the heavens. And to show the greater brilliance of the sun (the same book) says: He made the great (body) bright for the power of the day, and the small (body) bright for the power of the night, and (he has does) the stars. From which it is evident that for each power they are established, and one does not take its light from the other.

And the waxing and waning of the moon (is) like the entrance and exit (of a blade) through a sheath, say these wise men, and they give as a sign that it sometimes happens, when (the moon) is in its growth and in its fullness, around its vase it thickens, as if, through some small crack of holes, lights appeared.

And then of the darkening of the sun if the meeting of the moon was the cause, when the moon (it) darkens, what (obstacle) did it encounter? If they suppose a star to be the cause of this encounter, we do not see that a star so large is in the heavens that, meeting the moon, it could hide the moon; and there is no star lower than the moon, which, meeting it below, obscures it.

Moreover, if the moon could block out the light of the sun, then it would shine its light upon the earth, so that it would at least appear like a moon day, and not complete darkness.

9. But true is the word of Scripture which says: I will make the sun turn into darkness and the moon into blood; to show that he is the master of the

REFUTATIONS

luminous bodies, (the master) of lighting and darkening for the condemnation of the worshipers of the sun and the worshipers of the moon.

And it is not possible for the moon to descend to earth; as enchanters, having seen in time, by the command of God, a shape of a bloody moon, publish that the moon resembles the demon, (saying) that they will make the moon descend. It is not possible for this to be the case that the moon, which is larger than several worlds, is concentrated in a small place, it is not possible that (a woman) without a breast can suckle.

And what countless myriads of enchanters there are on earth! If each of them could bring down the moon, they would never give it (permission) to go to the heavens. But the moon never descends (on earth), this is obvious, since no one sees it descend or rise, and, if you pay close attention, the vase of the moon is lit little by little, until it is fully formed. If it were possible for the moon to descend, although no one saw it descend, yet everyone would see it ascend. But the luminous bodies are of such measure, as the divine books say, that they will be (destined) for signs, to times, and to days and to years.

Now, if the stars are (taken) as signs of heat or cold, it is not as living beings, but as appointed by God to this (office), so that none of God's creatures is unoccupied. And the wise men of Greece are blameworthy in that they followed and worshiped the creatures, and not the Creator.

10. And then, it is not (true), as they say, that the water surrounds the earth, but in the earth and on the earth are the waters; and beyond the earth there is nothing, not even water; which is evidenced by the Pillars of Hercules, on which it is written, they say, that * beyond this point no one has the audacity to go.

And the air is mixed with the waters and with the earth, and with the waters the air is mixed; this is evident from the reptiles, which in the waters suck the vitality from the air; and with the earth also the same air is mixed, when it makes rain and the sun gives, by the vapor which escapes from the heart of the earth, this seems obvious; and with the air also the fire is mixed, according to the lightning, which from the natural shock of the wind and the clouds springs up, this is evidently demonstrated; and then, if in a white glass you throw water into the sun, the brilliance of the sun, entering through the whiteness of the glass, and through the limpidity of the water penetrating through the air, gives rise to (the appearance of) fire; with the waters fire is mixed, according to the stones taken from the water, which are struck against each other, and (from which) we draw fire, this is obviously demonstrated; and at night, when you are by the sea, and you beat the water, flashes of light escape.

And the reptiles which are in the interior of the waters are composed of the four matters, namely: earth and water, air and fire, as also all the corporeal (beings) which are on the continent; for thus God composed the world. First, having made the four separate materials, then with them he composed everything. Of one creator all is the work, and he (alone) directs and maintains everything.

11. And not as the chief of their philosophers and the Peripatetics say one (single) unity, cause of everything, and Providence, that they do not say (emanated) from it (unity), but this providence would be a certain particular force, and as the cause of everything; (Pythagoras) draws it from one unit; if he admitted providence as born from this unity, he would form a beautiful and praiseworthy system; but, because from one being he causes causes to emanate, and from another (being) Providence, he is worthy of blame, and not of respect.

And then, by this very fact that he did not order sacrifice to the gods, he is praiseworthy. But because he did not openly preach that there is one God, and not many, he is very blameworthy.

Praiseworthy and very commendable is Pythagoras, because, to overcome passions and concupiscence, as for food, he lived as a religious man. But, because he gave (as certain) the transmutation of souls, of bodies into bodies, it is very reprehensible: as if the souls of the righteous dead passed into other pure bodies, or (into bodies) of non-filthy men or brutes, and that this came to them as a reward for good deeds; and (as if) the souls of sinners passed into the defiled bodies, whether of men, or of wild beasts, and of animals, and of reptiles, and that this happened to them as retribution for their evil deeds.

And (the order) not to eat meat, if, to deceive the passions of the body, he gave this order, he did good and (thing) just, but if, like filthy creatures he ordered to abstain from it , (it was) very bad; but evident are the reasons why he ordered not to eat the flesh of breathing animals; as if the divine breath was in their flesh, and that for this it was not necessary to eat the flesh of living (beings). This is also why the magicians first immolate, then kill the brutes, so that, having become insensible, the breath escapes from their bodies; and they do not know that they kill them twice, one by immolating them, the other by slitting their throats.

Likewise also, Pythagoras does not command the sacrifice of brutes to the gods, as if it were not necessary to sacrifice the gods to the gods; because the divine breath, he says, (is) in the brutes. And from this it is evident that he commands us to worship the earth, and not to sacrifice.

It was an extremely unworthy action to deem everything above the moon immortal. He shows that all these he considered as gods. And from there, supposing mortal (that which is) below, he indicated that fire, and air and earth, were beings living and dying, but not having the feeling of vitality, (fire, the air, the earth) do not take on the impression of death; what is proper to animate (beings) and not to inanimate (beings).

And this silence of five years which Pythagoras imposed on his new disciples, although it was an example of great patience, for they could ask for nothing but only be silent, was not very useful; for, if before the (appointed) time of five years, one of these disciples died, although (by dint of) having listened well and much he had become wise, he himself did not enjoy this wisdom, because he could not speak, and no one else (enjoyed it), because no one heard (speak) wisdom.

REFUTATIONS

And what is inconceivably stupid, then, they say, Pythagoras called himself God, which happened to him mainly out of pride, because he did not behave according to the words of the wise man who said that: * You might as well you will achieve greatness, you might as well keep yourself in humility.

12. But Plato, who admits God, and matter, and the idea in essence, shows that God is creator of forms, and not of natures. Hence the sects, having taken (this system), with it (Plato) falsely repeat that, as God was in essence, so also matter and idea, which is a particular property of the individual. As to God the skill was particular, the matter (was) material; (God) could only bring into forms the matter which was moving pell-mell, and not from what did not exist he brought everything into existence, as he can everything; which places on God (the reproach of) weakness, if he needed to borrow the material from another. In this way, (God) finds himself to be nothing more than the skillful workers, since, like them, he will need matter. And (Pythagoras) says the world is creature and destructible. And sometimes he and others say it is co-eternal with God.

If the world is creature and destructible, how could it be co-eternal with God? and, if it were co-eternal, as they say that, as the shadow of an individual never departs from him, so also the world never separates itself from God; if this is so, it is vain for them to say that this world is a destructible creature. But, if they could still advance this impiety that he who is the cause of the shadow must disappear. If then it is not so, for it is not, and the shadow must not disappear; then these stupidities are reprehensible.

And the souls (or breaths), if, because they are of the essence of God, were uncreated, and immortal, the three parts which (are) in them, where would they be from? (the part) reasonable, and the angry, and the concupiscible; for, although one (of these parts) is God, for he is the source of all rationality, but of anger and concupiscence, God, superior (to the passions), is free; for without needs, and without parts is God.

And if he himself, as they say, for greater perfection, a virgin came out of this world, how did he order others to put women in common, and not only to watch over his wife?

And why did he (Plato), like the first, consider the divine souls transmutable from body to body, even to reptiles and animals? His blasphemy will even (attack) nature in its impiety; as if he had half of himself in himself, and tormented his other half in reptiles and animals. Which is not (the fact) of that which is indivisible, indefinite, infringable and without parts.

And if, as they falsely say, many gods from one God had come forth, why should there not be many worlds, nor many heavens, nor many suns, nor many earths? But perhaps it is insignificant gods that (God) has drawn from him, and of insignificant gods what use would they be?

13. As for the Stoics, who think only of bodies, looking at the apparent world, they believed that everything was body, and they considered the apparent world as God. These sectarians know this from the philosophers, they did not want to put into their minds a very understandable point, nor to learn it from others, it is that there is a power which moves things apparent, and that we must look at the mover as God, and not at moving things.

Now, some of them, from the essence of fire, speak of the nature of the world, (and this) to make the sun appear (as a marvel) even more astonishing, and nature finally (as) even more vehement; and, considering that we can contemplate everything through intelligence, for this they believed intelligence to be God (himself); as the breath of the heavens, and of the earth, and of all (that which is) in the heavens and on the earth. They took the luminous (bodies) for his eyes. (These people), in their outrageous stupidity, are not even worthy of a response.

And bodies, like the stars, they consider perishable, and souls transmutable from body to body, which they cannot demonstrate, neither they nor others

REFUTATIONS

more eminent than them; because they all tell fables. And although half came to the truth, they did not stand in the truth.

14. (As for the) Epicureans, they believe the world constitutes itself; as if first the atoms were walking. Like, when a ray (of the sun) enters through the window, atoms appear in this ray; such, they say, the offending and indivisible bodies were first, then thickened (successively), the world was formed by aggregation; and (they say) that there is neither God nor providence which guides the world. These people, whom philosophers denigrate, other sects do not esteem at all. It is of them of whom the apostle says that: * Without God they circulated in the world. So extravagant was their obstinacy, to the point that, from such a large troop of gods, these philosophers did not retain a god. Do you see that the fact of such audacity dominating these possessed (of error), went so far as to (give birth or) remove atheism from the world.

15. Under Saruch was, they say, the beginning of paganism; from which it is evident that up to this time one was worshiping God, and that the Church of God was (established) from the beginning of the world. Whereupon David, being instructed by the Holy Spirit, offered prayers (to God, saying): Remember thy Church which thou hast established from the beginning.

But, although paganism entered the world, the worship of God was not entirely lacking; and this is evident, since Abraham, having gone from the land of the heathen, met worshipers of God. Melchizedek, priest of the Most High God, is never appointed priest without his people; and Abimelech who, by (the power of) God alone, spoke with Abraham, and not by (the power of) demons. And Job's friends, and Elijah, by (the power of) Almighty God alone, spoke with him.

Thus, God never left this world without testimony; as the prophet, under Judaism, said, as in the face of God, that: In all places they throw incense, and they offer sacrifices in my name; to show that in all ages there were worshipers of God who confounded the idolaters.

16. But, they say, why was the coming of Christ delayed (so long), and so many generations were lost without the knowledge of God?

If there had not been preachers of the worship of God sent throughout the centuries, perhaps there would be occasion for such discourses; but as (God) did not cease to give testimony, let them blame themselves, the unbelievers, and not God!

Christ did not come in the infancy of the world, because milk was useful to children, and not solid food, nor (he did not come) in his fiery youth, when the worship of demons was widespread. But first he lifted up the world through (the means of) the prophets, as with milk, and then he came to give his accomplished doctrine; for no one gives the child solid food, nor reveals to him great mysteries, nor speaks to him serious language, until he comes to perfect age.

As the apostle, taking upon himself all the traits of humanity says: * When I was a child, like a child I thought; but, when I was a man, I left childhood there, to show that Christ came into the world in the completed age (of the world), in his perfect knowledge, as in this world one can arrive. But, to the enjoyment of this knowledge, Christ invited himself and others, saying that: * Now we know little, but when the consummation comes, we will see face to face.

From which it is evident that, over everything, God is powerful, and for everything He is sufficient. He could even rather, in the first ages of eternity, make the world, but he wanted this way, so as not to do it either too soon or too late, but when it was appropriate and convenient, lest, by doing it too early, created beings do not harm him, by thinking that they were co-eternal to him, and also lest, by doing it late, we (have from him) suspicions of weakness, of indecisive projects, of first, and medial, and last thoughts.

Moreover, man, whom God wanted to make heir of everything, he did not do it before (making) the inheritance; but first (he made) the heavens and the earth, the waters and the fire, and the air and the grass, and the plants and the wild beasts, and the brutes and the birds; first the house, then the keeper of the house; first the possessions, then the possessor; first the slaves, then the master, lest, when afterwards the beings of whom (man) became the prince came, he should conceive sinful ideas (as) if they were his creatures. But when, first, he sees them made, he will take into his mind (this idea) that, it is a power which made them, and gave them (to him), (and placed) under his hand, and let man not think of giving himself the honor of this glorification, but (let him offer it) to his Lord-creator who freely gave him all this.

Likewise the coming of his Son, (God) prepared it at the time when he knew that it must be useful. And if a doctor, according to the different diseases, presents different remedies to his patients, so that (the remedy) which suits the beginning of the disease, it is administered at the beginning, and (that the remedy which suits) at the medial period , (it is administered) in the middle (of the disease), and that the remedy (which is suitable) for the old period of the disease, (it is administered) immediately afterwards; how much more does the sovereign author, by whom all means of invention are provided, do what he does in due time; not by (the effect of) a first and second and last thought, but at the same time, according to his will, he accomplishes the work of his products, and not as a result his will is born; but, as by prescience he knows everything, while a thing does not yet exist, (he knows) how he must do it, and in what time, and for what needs; he does nothing confusedly that he later regrets, and (makes him) destroy his own creations. He needs no one, he takes nothing from anyone, and expects nothing from anyone; but he has in himself sufficient power to do, and to establish everything, and to preserve (it) intact. He has no one associated with him, as a brother, or as a companion, or as a foreign cooperator; but (he has) only his power and his wisdom which is born of his essence, and (is) co-eternal to him, and the spirit of his nature which (proceeds) from him, and is always with him, indestructible and without division possible.

17. From all this it is evident that no ὕλη, that is to say matter, was with God, from which the wise men of Greece say that he made the creatures, 'it (matter) evils have entered the world, as say the sects who have taken reasons from them (to) deify matter, and place God opposed to God. And no one else was the creator of evils, as the wise men falsely relate (saying) that Araman created evils;

REFUTATIONS

but one God is creator, (creator) of goods, and not of evils, and eternal creator; for, while he had not yet made the creatures, he had in his mind, through foreknowledge, the plan of the composition of the creatures. And there was never (a time) when he was not creator, because he had within himself the power sufficient for the production of all.

And there were many reasons (before) God for him to come and make creatures. First of all, the science of truth should not be left inert, for fear that, like a powerless being, God himself would be found, for not having been able to make the creatures, for which he had within himself the know-how. by (the effect of) his preconceived science; secondly, as (God) is beneficent by nature, he had no right to keep his beneficence useless. And there were many other similar reasons for God, why he gave the beginning to the composition of the world.

As someone, if he knows the art of certain things, whether of music, or of medicine, or of carpentry, and by effects he does not show the truth (of his talents), in vain he has all the details of science, from which (it follows that) he himself does not enjoy them, and does not show others the knowledge of his art; in the same way also whoever would be beneficent, if his beneficence is not enjoyed, to whom would his beneficence serve? because of beneficence virtue is such: (it exists) when others enjoy it. If there is no one who enjoys beneficence, what use would there be (to derive) from beneficence?

Likewise, God, who had skill in him, consummate art, if he had not made creatures, would think in vain of having skill, when there were no subjects which resulted from his skill. Moreover, his beneficence would not show itself as beneficence, if he had not created the creatures who benefit from his beneficence; but it is so beneficent that, not only has he granted to his creatures their creation, but also (the favor) of enjoying the joys of his perfections.

Then, if God had not made creatures, no one would even know that he is God, unless there were beings there who possessed the power of knowledge (of God). From which (it follows that), as God wanted to bring us to his knowledge, and he himself is (there to) show it, he has disposed his creatures to present to them the knowledge (of his person), so that they may enjoy his beneficence. And he made the functions of the world for man, (proper) for the service of all necessary things; and man, (he did it) for his glory, that he might glorify his Lord, and know his goodness.

And thus God was never empty of creation, because he always had (traces), painted in the mind (the creatures) that he had to make, and, as it was not only in will and in thoughts he had this power, for this, in order to manifest his will and his thoughts, he brought to light his creatures, so that his power appeared, and his creatures enjoyed his beneficence.

Now, let no one be able to believe the world constituted of itself, nor anything (pre-existing) with God, so as not to overthrow the greatness of his power! But to all he granted being, (to all beings) which were not before. Why would we want to suppress his power, and regard him only (as) the skillful implementer of some matter, and not, (as) of nothing leading to being all things? There was nothing co-eternal with God, nor any matter from which he took and composed his creatures; but he himself is creator of all natures; and not only does he arrange the forms, mix the essence of essential beings, but he is also the author and creator of the existence of existing beings.

Such (is what) men concerning God must say, and of these stories be the historians. By this God is glorified, and men do not harm themselves.

But according to the merits of God, (who are the men) who will be worthy to be historians of God, except the friends of God, who, for love of him, have despised the life of the world, and, preferring death for the hope of life which is with God, have given themselves up to the loss of the body, (loss) from which is (result) the salvation of souls?

Now, in vain the wise men of Greece strive to discourse on God, because they have not been able to distinguish the creator and the creatures, (these wise men) who, (reason) obscured by the darkness of demons, imagined introducing several lineages of countless gods.

Like Hesiod, a certain wise man among them, counted many generations of gods, and Homer the rhapsodic, following Hesiod, in pompous speech repeats the same errors, and many other philosophers, with words fabulous extravagant, promise to fulfill God's story; (these people), who do not know God, and do not know how to separate the creator from the creatures, how do they think to talk about God? and above all the one whom they regard (as) wiser than all (the others), Plato who, on the subject of God, and on the subject of souls, and on the subject of creatures wanted to speak.

And now against Plato we must fight with bold words, (against Plato) who (more) than all the Greek philosophers appears to be worshiper of the true God; for he finds himself not knowing God, nor the creation of creatures; for when we have traced the passions of this famous man, and then removed him from the eyes of his dupes, we will then show who God is, and what his creatures are.

One thing that Plato especially considers unspeakable is that God has always been and had no creatures. I like Plato's desire to seek God, and I do not praise his pride.

BOOK FOUR
REFUTATION OF THE SECT OF MARCION

1. Marcion, misguided, introduces the stranger against the god of laws, admitting with him also ὕλη, (matter) in essence, and three heavens. In one, say (the Marcionites) dwells the stranger, and in the second the god of laws, and in the third his forces, and on earth ὕλη, and they call it power of the earth.

And thus (God) disposes of the world and the creatures, as the laws say; but also Marcion adds that in community with ὕλη, (God) did everything he did; and, as if female and woman (fit) for marriage were ὕλη, (he says): And after having made the world, God ascended with his forces into the heavens, and ὕλη and his children remained on the earth; and they took each his principality, ὕλη on earth, and the god of laws in heaven.

And the god of laws, having seen that the world was beautiful, thought of making man there; and, having descended near ὕλη to the earth, he said: Give me of your clay, and on my part I will give the breath, and we will make man according to our likeness. Ὕλη, having given him of his earth, God shaped it and breathed into it the breath, and Adam was (created) with the vital breath; and for this he was called Adam, because of slime he was made. And having created Adam and his wife, and having placed them in the earthly paradise, as the laws say, they went continually, and obeyed him; and they were joyful in him as in their common son.

And, says (Marcion,) the lord of the laws, who was the master of the world, having seen that Adam was (a being) excellent and worthy of service, contrived how he could remove him from ὕλη, and attach him to his party. Having taken him aside, he said to him: Adam, I am God, and there is no other; and besides me, let there be no other God for you! If you have any God other than me, know that you will die a (certain) death. And when he had said this to him, and Adam remembered the name of death, struck with terror, he began to separate himself a little from ὕλη.

REFUTATIONS

And ὕλη, having come to give him orders according to his custom, saw (clearly) that Adam did not obey him, but thoughtfully kept himself apart, and no longer approached ὕλη. Then astonished in his mind, ὕλη understood that the Lord of creatures had set ambushes for him. He says: from the orifice of the spring, corrupted is its water. What is this? Adam has not yet multiplied in generations, and (God) has taken him away from me by the name of his divinity. Since he hated me, and did not keep the treaty with me; I will make many gods, and I will fill the world with their being, so that it may seek who God is, and not find Him.

And ὕλη made, they say, many idols, and called them gods, and filled the world with them. And swallowed up was the name of God, which is (the name) of the lord of creatures, among the names of many gods, and (God) was nowhere to be found; and the posterity (of Adam) went astray with these (gods), and did not preserve (the true God), for ὕλη drew all to himself, and did not give even one of them permission to cultivate (God). Then, they say, the master of the creatures was angry because they left him and obeyed ὕλη. And one after another, (the souls) which came out of the bodies, he threw them in anger into hell; and he cast Adam into hell because of the tree; and thus he cast into hell all (men) up to twenty-nine generations.

What, they say, the good and strange God, who sat in the third heaven, having seen, that so many generations were lost and persecuted, between two cunning beings, the master of creatures, and ὕλη, was moved with pity for the (unfortunate) who have fallen into fire and torture; he sent his Son to save them, and to take the likeness of a slave, and to appear in the form of a man among the children of the God of laws. Heal, says God, their leprosy, resurrect their dead, open (the eyes of) their blind, and do in them the greatest healings freely; finally, until the master of creatures sees you, becomes jealous of you, and places you on the cross; and then, at your death, you will descend into hell, and you will bring out (the victims); for the hells are not accustomed to receiving life in their midst. And for this you will be lifted up on the cross, that you may be like the dead; and the deep will open its mouth (to) receive you, and you will enter into the midst of it, and you will make it empty.

REFUTATIONS

And when (God) had raised (his Son) on the cross, they say, (he) descended into hell and emptied them; and, having withdrawn the souls, he carried them to the third heavens to his Father. And the lord of creatures (all) angry, in anger tore his cloak and the veil of his palace; and he darkened his sun, and he clothed his world black, and he sat mourning for sorrow.

Then a second time, Jesus having descended in the form of his divinity to the master of creatures, entered into judgment with him because of his death; and the Lord of the world, seeing the divinity of Jesus, knew that he was another God than he, and Jesus said to him: My judgment is upon you, and let no one be judge between us, but let your laws which you have written (pronounce). And when he had presented the laws, Jesus said to him: Have you not written in your laws that whoever kills will die, and that whoever sheds the blood of the righteous, his blood will be shed? And (the master of the world) said: Yes, I have written it. And Jesus said to him: Deliver yourself into my hands, that I may kill you and shed your blood, as you killed me and shed my blood; for I am righteous more than you, and I have done immense benefits to your creatures. And Jesus began to enumerate the benefits he did to the creatures (of the master of the world).

And when the master of creatures saw that (Jesus) had overcome him, he did not know what to say; because, by his very laws he was condemned, and found no answer to give; for he was liable to death, in retaliation for the death of (Jesus). Then, throwing himself into supplications, he implored (Jesus, saying): Because I have sinned, and have put you to death without knowing it, for I did not know that you were God, but I believed to be a man, I give you as an atonement all those who will believe in you; lead them wherever you want. Then Jesus, having left the master of creatures, took and ravished Paul, and discovered redemption to him, and sent him to preach (and announce) that: We are redeemed (by redemption), and whoever believes in Jesus has been sold by the just to (be good).

This is the beginning of Marcion's sect, leaving aside many other trivialities. Not all know this, few (of his disciples) know it, and transmit this teaching from mouth to mouth to one another. They say: The stranger has redeemed us

REFUTATIONS

from the lord of creatures, but how and with what has he redeemed us? (This is) what not everyone knows.

2. Response. Just as the blessed apostle says: The wisdom of this world is foolishness before God. What do they take, or what do they mix, or, by whose word do they speak? If, for Marcion, true is the god of laws, from whom he supposes (emanate) the creatures, the foreigner whom he introduces as his auxiliary should not covet his creatures, although they were in torments or at rest: for, if he were God, he himself was worthy to make creatures, and (should) not covet the creatures of another. But, as he did nothing, it is evident that he was not at all; because, if he was like God, he must have all power in him. And if, of himself, he did not have such wisdom, at least, by contemplating the creator of the world, (he would have known) how to learn art from him; but if he could not become like the (creator of the world), at least (it was necessary) that he be like ὕλη who was lying on the ground, and be a participant in the creation of the creator. But it is evident that (the doctrines of) this sect are nonsense, and not truth.

But first, to admit the god of laws, and ὕλη equal to him, (it is) a system stolen from the philosophers, who impute impotence to God, saying that: He could not do anything out of nothing, but (that he drew everything) from the material present (before him). And, although in a thousand ways in the name of the stranger and of his son Jesus, whom they call benefactor, they take refuge, they are not separated from the pagans; for as these say (that there are) many gods, so also these preach the same gods. And they are liable to death a thousand times over; for, created by the god of laws, in the name of the stranger they encourage themselves like felons, (in the name of the stranger) who among men is not adored; for the servant of the king of kings cannot devote himself to Caesar, nor the servant of Caesar to devote himself to the Sassanid; otherwise, he is found worthy of capital punishment.

Then these (the pagans) say (that there are) lines of many gods; and these (the Marcionites) of the marriage of the god of laws and ὕλη (or matter), they say procreate all creatures. And what are they (therefore) more than the Magi who, by marriage, assume (issue) all their gods? Let them therefore show what spirit

REFUTATIONS

gave them these laws; for the Holy Spirit, which spoke to the prophets and apostles, they have denied.

3. But Paul, they say, was caught up into the third heaven, and heard these unspeakable words which we preach.

This is (what) Paul says: (Words) that it is not necessary for man to speak. Now (as for Marcion, if he is a man, to him these words were unspeakable; he who, indeed, is a man, is worse than all men. Leaving (aside) the truth of the (holy) Spirit. , he sits in (the error of the) fables that he spouts. And so possessed is he of the satanic spirit, that he dares to sort through the precepts of the Holy Spirit, extract part of the Gospel, and leave a part of it (as a thing) useless; in the same way, (he wrote) apostolic epistles. The Old Testament he denied entirely, as if it were given by (a foolish being), and not by (a being) good.

And the apostle said: Unspeakable are the words which I have heard. And Marcion said: I have heard them. Now, is it the apostle, who believes these unspeakable words, (that we) must listen to, or Marcion who, rejecting them, puts them into nothingness?

4. Then, if eternal were the god of laws, he would also have to be prescient and omniscient, and if he were not prescient and omniscient, then he was not perfect. Behold, he appears perfect, because he made the heavens and all the earth, and not only one heaven, but two (heavens) and many forces. And he who is enough for all this, how could he not know that there is someone above him of whom he would have some suspicion? and, if he knew it, why did he not fortify his place, so that there would be no entry for the adversary who stood there, and caused his creatures to revolt against him?

And then the good (being) that they call thus, if, as they say, by nature was good, and that wickedness was not in him, since he thought of (doing) good to others, why did he think does he (do) harm to himself, to be saddened by his creatures? for the latter continually makes men, and the latter, by always turning them away from himself, makes them miserable; which is the work not of the good, but of the bad.

5. Then again, whoever they say is righteous, if he was truly righteous, having divided his principalities, made for himself the two heavens, and to ὕλη and his sons left only the earth, how was he (possible) that, another time, coveting his world, he said: Give me your clay, and I, on my part, will give the breath, and we will make man according to our likeness; what is the work, not of the just, of coveting the world of another, but rather the work of an unjust (being)?

Or else ὕλη (matter), how was she struck by this idea, once separated from the (god of laws), of having community with him again, of tricking herself, of giving entry to the stranger into his world, so that he made Adam and his companion there, (Adam) who sometimes gave hands to this one, and sometimes to that one?

But also the master of creatures, how do they even call him the just? for, first, as they say, he did not do something alone, but (he and ὕλη) did in common what they did; and, secondly, of common materials they made man, and both together they rejoiced in him; for if, as they say, only the god of laws was just, it is evident that he would give orders of justice to ὕλη, and if only wicked were ὕλη, it would be necessary for him to give (to the god of laws) only opinions of nastiness.

And how did it happen that both rejoiced in man, who unlike each other gave orders? One (of the orders) of good, as (to be) good, and the other (of the orders) of evil, as (to be) evil; for neither the righteous, since he was just by nature, can it be (proper) to give evil orders, nor the wicked, since he was wicked by nature, to give orders for good.

But still being joyful, where did this disposition come from for the wicked, (he) who was always gloomy and morose? Or, cunning, (where this thought came from) to the righteous, who naturally was very just, and animated by thoughts of equity, about whom it was not possible to think (and believe) only his (creature), man a creature (made in) common? but, as righteousness, it was a duty for him to think that: As we have made man together, we must also enjoy in common in him; but (it is) not like being infinitely just, but like being cunning and suspicious (that), having taken man aside, he seduced him (by saying that): I am God, and he there is no other, except me. And it suited Adam to say that: When you wanted to make me, he was another God, when you asked him for earth, and, now, how do you want me to think that I am only yours; Who would be God alone, and there is no other?

But perhaps (Adam) was frightened by the announcement of death, which he nevertheless suffered, whether he wanted it or not. And he did not know this, (the god of laws), that ὕλη was setting trap after trap for him, swallowing up his unique name in the midst of many gods, that he was causing a scandal to man; of this damage was not the last sinner, but (the cause was) the one who first deceived; for, if he had not shown him such an art, ὕλη would not have imagined it; but he himself was the tutor of his own traps, and of the deceitfulness of ὕλη.

6. When he saw that no one worshiped him, he made mortal men; and those whose souls came out of their bodies, he threw one after the other into hell.

Now, rather than throwing them into hell, why didn't he who deceived them throw him into hell? Is it because he couldn't defeat him? If then ὕλη was more dominant than him, why did ὕλη give him his dupes to torment?

But still the just, if he really were just, should not henceforth make men; for he knew that ὕλη must deceive them; but, as righteousness, he had to think (of this): What use is there for me to make (creatures), while another turns them away from me? Moreover, tormenting them was not fair, since he knew that, through the actions of others, they were sinning.

7. But yet another thing, which they say, is more impious than all (the rest): that, when the good (principle), which sat in the third heavens, saw the souls of these twenty-nine generations tormented in Gehenna, sympathizing with their

fate, he sent Jesus, his son, to take the likeness of the slave, and appear in the form of men.

If he was so compassionate, then why did he not send his son to save (men); but (he sent him) only after (having seen) the souls of twenty-nine generations tormented in Gehenna.

But first, to say three heavens, where did Marcion (come from this idea)? for Moses says two heavens; but, as the sectaries have exaggerated in everything, so also in this (point); for one says ten heavens, another seven, Marcion three; and, according to the holy books, they want to establish their error, (maintaining) that the (holy) books speak of the heavens and the heavens of heavens, in a manifold manner.

When sectarians are not restrained by anyone, outside of the holy books, they go wild; and then, when they are in danger, in the holy books they take refuge; but heavens, and heavens of heavens, we find (these words) in Scripture, because in the language of the Hebrews we cannot say sky, as in the Syriac language (we do not say) water, or sky; but one is said in the plural.

And hence it is evident that by the Septuagint (it was) translated (thus) into Greek, they say: From the beginning God made heaven and earth, thus showing (that it is a question of) 'one (only) sky; and in the Syriac language, as one cannot say sky, it is said: From the beginning God made the element heaven and the element earth. Although we cannot say in the singular a sky, however by saying *hatn*, that is to say element, the translation indicates as an element of a sky. Moreover, the firmament, which is separated from the waters, the Septuagint translated sky; from which it is evident that the upper heaven and the inner heaven are two heavens, and not three or more.

But they say, Paul said that: he was caught up as (as he was) unto the third heavens, and they do not know this that it is not even certain that (Paul) says unto the third heavens, or up to the third part of the many parts of a heaven, and above all that, without article, it says which is; for he does not say up to the third heaven, but up to the third of heaven, said in the singular. So Paul gives (as) acceptance, that in a third part of heaven Paul was caught up. Therefore, after this he said that he was caught up as (he was) in the earthly Paradise; and the earthly Paradise was not in the third heavens, nor anywhere in the heavens, but on earth. This is what they themselves testify, saying that: they made man, and placed him in Paradise, which (Paradise) is on earth, and not in heaven.

But the elevation is also called heavens, as when the Scripture says * The birds of the heavens, and the dews of the heavens, the clouds, and the winds of the heavens; not that (all this) is in the heavens, but because it is in the elevation, (the birds, etc.,) are called (birds, etc.) of the heavens. Moreover, of the trees which are at any height, we say that they are lifted up to the heavens; and smoke, (we say that) it mixes with the sky. According to this example, we must understand this expression of Paul: third heavens.

Begin with the first, and go down to the second, and arrive at the third air which, by the (holy) books, is called heaven, and you find what the blessed apostle says: And he heard unspeakable words which no one should utter. Although the Apostle was a chosen vessel, yet he was companion of Peter, companion in the yoke of the sons of thunder, co-preacher with Barnabas. How had it (happened) that he alone had to hear and utter unspeakable words, and his companions, no (this was not given)? Were there not then the same graces in all, and one and the same spirit in them? But unspeakable (were) these words; not that they were possible for him to say, and, for his other companions, unspeakable; but, according to what, in his first epistle to the Corinthians, the apostle says: What eye has not seen, nor ear heard, nor has it entered the heart of man, (this is) what God has prepared for his friends.

It is also (good) to hear thus: Not that I alone was worthy of this mystery, I who am the last of the apostles, but, although Peter, (he) who is the chief of the apostles, sees this he cannot repeat; although he hears it, he cannot tell it; for unspeakable are these (things) and above the intelligence and language of men. And for this, says the apostle, although I have seen, I cannot relate; whatever I have heard, I cannot say it again.

Then which God, of the creatures of which God was the support, whether (these creatures were in torment or in peace; or, as for the passage of Jesus in his world, how did (this God) not know it himself, (neither him) nor any of his troops, nor of the others, (no more than they knew) the exit of Jesus from (his domains)? And if, touching him, as (being) God, they could not know anything, of so many souls that he attracted near them in his heavens, how did they not perceive some noise; or the guards of the prisons of these souls how did they not (achieve) advice to their master? But it is obvious that these speeches are vain, and these stories incredible.

8. And if in likeness only Jesus was made man, and in form only were his cross, and his torments, and his death, then salvation was not wrought. But also, why was he saving someone else's creatures, creatures that he had not made? (for) it is the work, not of a good (being), but of an evil (being) to penetrate by stealth, to enter into the house of another, and to lay ambushes for him.

But we will still ask this: Was Jesus (a being) corporeal or incorporeal? If they say that he was incorporeal, let them listen to this: If Jesus came (as being) incorporeal, and here below, as they say, he did not put on a body, it is evident that he gave nothing, and took nothing, and died not, and saved not. And absurd is this saying of Marcion, that of the blood of Jesus we are the price; for his blood was not shed, nor were men redeemed, because they say that in form and appearance were his cross, and his death, and not in reality; and the Jews refute them, they who, until today, are assured that their fathers put Jesus on the cross. From which it is obviously demonstrated that, not in appearance Jesus was raised on the cross, but in reality; for of our true (or the truth of our) resurrection he gave his own resurrection as an example.

9. And if, as they say, Jesus asked for the laws of the just as judge and mediator (of his conduct), according to these very laws, he is already liable to death, since, before his crucifixion, he (captured) a lot of people. Not only (he did this), but he chose many other men from among them, and sent them to make disciples, and to draw them to him.

REFUTATIONS

And not only (he did) all this, but also he put on their own strength to trample under foot the forces of their master, and threw the sword and division into his house, and kindled fire against his creatures; (he went) so far as to abrogate, to destroy his laws, in the days of John the Baptist, to the extent of evangelizing (or publishing) his own reign, sending everywhere many preachers to preach (his faith), many reapers to reap what he himself had not sown; and this, when no one had yet sinned against him, nor had he been put to the cross, nor had he shed his blood, he devastated the house (of the Lord of creatures), and ruined his kingdom, and he remained silent, and did no harm to (his enemy).

And how, they say, (did it happen) that, by his crucifixion, Jesus redeemed Marcion, since all these multitudes, while he was not yet lifted up on the cross, he reconciled to himself?

But they say (these multitudes), he won them as the price of healings. He healed the sick, and he cleansed the lepers; he raised the dead, he restored the paralyzed, and he caused the demons to flee. And is there a doctor (who), when he cures the son of an individual, does not receive a reward? but, as the main price of his cure, demands his cured patient, and we will record here that, (for him), his cured patients were (attached) to him because of his benefits. As for those whom he did not heal, why did he detach them from their master? Which is the fact, not of a good (being), but of a cunning (being).

And how could (Jesus) ask for these laws as judges? (the laws) of him to whom, before his death, he had done so much harm in his house, especially since he knew that these laws condemned him to death and did not justify him. Now if in the form of an Israelite he came to his house, yet he must be condemned, for it was written in these laws * that every Jew who breaks the laws shall be killed, and he who does not be circumcised, and will not keep the Sabbath, die. And (Jesus) broke the laws, ruined religion; he was (therefore) condemned by the laws, and, if in the form of other nations he came to (the Jews), previously they were ordered to exterminate the foreigners, and not to spare them. And then on strangers and guests this order weighed: * If they do not keep the worship of the laws, let them die a certain death. Thus, according to all laws, he was punishable by death.

REFUTATIONS

Is there anyone who would enter furtively into the house of his companion (to) steal something, (and who, caught in the act, would not be condemned to death? Or is there someone who, coming near, disposes the sons of another person, or his slaves to insolence and perversity, (and who, if one comes upon him, is not made to lose the head? Or is there anyone who, entering as a spy, furtively spies on the kingdom of another, a (once) known spy, not be promptly exterminated?

Likewise, also Jesus, before his crucifixion, did much damage in the house of the righteous, and, according to the laws which he asked for judges, he found himself liable to a thousand deaths; for, (like) a stranger coming into another's house, he brought upon him (suffer) the greatest disasters, broke his laws, the prophets, and proclaimed his own kingdom.

Who was it that could do such great things, except the Lord of all, who said: All things have been given to me by my Father? From which it is evident that, not as a stranger for squandering, but by a father (all things to him) was given, and as Lord of the laws he made the laws to cease; and, before being lifted up on the cross, he showed his kingdom.

O fools! how have you not understood that the Father of Jesus is the master of everything, by the very fact that he gave everything into his hands? He is the master of the world, and not the one you think, and who was not even; for whoever besides Him is called God, is not naturally God. And there are many other (things) by which it is demonstrated that our Lord came among his own, and not among strangers; and he and his Father are one (and the same) master of the world; and furthermore, by (the example of the) wounded man who, while going down from Jerusalem to Jericho, was wounded by bandits, it is demonstrated that Christ was not a stranger to the wounded man, but a neighbor, doctor. As also he himself said to the Pharisee: * You have judged right (and just). And by (the example of) the sheep and the silver coin, which were lost and were found, it is evident that to his own people he came, and not to strangers.

REFUTATIONS

10. Then this other word of the apostle, which is so rightly said, they overthrow. When (says the apostle) * he shall have destroyed all kingdoms and principalities, for he must reign, so that his enemies may be put under his feet. And they say that the ruler of the world destroys himself and his world in eternity.

O fools! if in his hand is (the power to) build up and (to) break, and he breaks his world because it becomes old and obsolete, why does he not make another new and more beautiful than that -this? If, when the world did not exist, he knew how to meditate on it, and to do it through his word; now that he has learned and been informed that there is another foreign world more beautiful, more excellent than his own, how will he not make one more perfect than this? so that people from abroad envy his world, because of its beauty and splendor; for, as he was (enough) powerful (to) make his first (world), so, if he wishes, he is (enough) powerful (to) make another more excellent than this one. And he, who is thus powerful, why should he reduce himself to being a stool under the feet of another? and will he not make his world new and more beautiful than the first, and he would reign there in eternity?

But if the stranger prevents him, and if (the stranger) is so strong that he can prevent it; therefore, he is not the master of everything, as he himself says, but the slave of another domination.

Or (well), from where will you show that the God of laws must break his world? If it is because it is written in the prophets that the heavens will be rolled up like parchment, and the earth like wax will melt; but he also wrote, in his prophecies: I will make new heavens and a new earth. Hence it is evident, according to the prophecy, that he would break this (world), but make a new one, as you yourself have testified.

But again, to this other question, give an answer. Who is he who will break his power and his dominion? And do you not know, according to the apostle, that Christ overthrows the powers, and puts all his enemies under his feet? And not this one you are talking about, who is not even, and has done nothing and is

REFUTATIONS

doing (nothing); but Our Lord and his Father, who are (enough) powerful (to) do all things, and subdue all enmities under their feet.

11. And then, if the stranger was powerful enough, as Marcion says, to free souls from these torments, why did he not by force put his hand (on it), and attract not the souls of these victims? But, first, he gave (as) permission for them to be tormented, then he released them (from pain). And this, not with boldness, but with (fear and) suspicion, and by redemption with his blood.

But, they say, (God) did this, because of his mercy. Having seen the souls of the victims tormented in hell, he sent his Son to save them. If (Jesus) saved them; the last, what will they be, (these souls) who must fall into hell? If by mercy (God) did what he did, why did he not keep the coming of his Son until the end of the world, and then send (this Son); for, (then), he had mercy on all, and (from the abyss) drew them (all) to life, rather than hastening to send (this Son) into the midst of the ages, and (then) he it is not possible for the last ones who fell (into the abyss) to come out; because now their persecutor is on his guard.

But these (people) are very misguided, and they have forgotten that there is no bad tree that produces good fruit: and that grapes are not gathered from thorns, nor figs from bush, and his contains his.

And yet another thing they say, that the underworld does not contain life; for this, (Jesus) went up on the cross, so that, descending as dead, hell would receive him.

Now therefore shall no one be sent there alive, neither sinful men, nor Satan, nor the demons of Satan alive. If this is so, hell does not receive them.

Or Jesus as dead, where did he go? is it in the tomb of the earth, which the Scripture calls hell, and there are not the souls, nor the fire which torments them; and if they say that he went into hell as dead, there is no ground for their discourse, for the Apostle does not give (to believe) that Jesus died two deaths,

REFUTATIONS

but one. only (death), which he suffered bodily, (the death) of the cross, and was subjected to the death of the cross; and (the Apostle) does not say that another judged him and cast him into hell, but that his Father delivered him to death, and then he delivered himself as a ransom for many through death of the body, and not by the torments of the soul.

12. But, so strongly contrary, they say, are the laws of the just to the graces of Jesus, that there happiness is given to the rich, and misery to the poor; here happiness to the poor, and misfortune to the rich; here (the righteous) says: Do not kill; and there, Jesus said: He who becomes angry with his companion unjustly, is liable to Gehenna; here (the righteous) says: Do not fornicate; and there, (Jesus) says that: He who looks at a woman out of lust has already fornicated in his heart; here (the righteous) says: Do not swear in vain, but pay to the Lord (the price of) your oaths; and there (Jesus) said: Do not swear at all.

And now how are these laws and graces contrary to each other? for Abraham, because he received strangers and the poor, was called a friend of God; and Christ says that: The poor into Abraham's bosom is gone, and the rich into the torments of the fire. Christ gives happiness to the poor and the merciful, (saying) that they will find mercy. And the God of laws shows so much mercy that the beast of an enemy fallen under the load, he does not want to be abandoned, whether (the master) is of the people (Jewish) or of a foreign nation; and the kid (still fed) on the mother's milk, he does not want to be roasted, and the hen sitting on her eggs or on her young, (he does not want to be taken together) ; there God says: You will love your companion as yourself; and here (Jesus) says: You shall love the Lord your God with all your heart, and you shall love your companion as yourself; for on these two commandments depend the laws and the prophets. And he said: * I have not come to dissolve the laws and the prophets, but to fulfill them.

Now how could he be contrary to the laws who came to fulfill the laws and the prophets? And he said to the leper, whom he had purified: * Go, offer sacrifice for your purification, as Moses commanded in his laws. And to the lawyer who asked him * what must I do, that I may inherit eternal life? (Jesus) said: * You know the commandments of the laws: and asked again, what (are these) commandments? He said: Do not fornicate, do not steal, do not kill. By this he made it evident that not contrary to the laws (was what) he taught, but (well) in conformity with these (laws).

Then, not losing your temper is in no way contrary to not killing, but extremely consistent; because, if someone does not lose his temper, he does not conceive the work of assassination. Likewise also not coveting (the flesh), is in no way contrary to not fornicating, but even better; for if anyone does not covet (the flesh), he is not inclined to the work of fornication; and not swearing at all is in no way opposed to not perjuring oneself, but (it is) a very correlative thing; because, if someone is not accustomed to (swear often), he never swears falsely. There, as (men) swore in the name of idols, (God) said: Pay (or do) to (the name of) the Lord your oaths. He said (again): By me you will swear, (by me) who am the living (being), and do not swear by (the name of) idols which are not (beings) living. Here, to make his disciples perfect, Christ says: Do not swear at all, but let the yes be yes for you, and the no, no; and what is more than that is evil. If what is more than yes and no is evil, how much more (does evil) he who swears falsely in the terrible name (of God)!

And then, by (the precept of) not getting carried away, and not coveting (the flesh, precept) which Jesus taught, it is evident that he considers the god of laws so much for God, that he strengthens his words in the Gospel, and they exaggerate (saying that) Jesus teaches the opposite of these (words). Likewise also, regarding food, in the Old and New Testaments we find that they are given by God for the maintenance (of life). There, (God) said: * Kill and eat every brute and edible birds. And here (Jesus) says that: * Whatever enters through a man's mouth does not defile him, but whatever comes out of the mouth, that defiles a man. And of all (food) the product is one (and the same thing), the flesh. And if some foods were impure, first (Jesus) would not have eaten them himself, and then would not have ordered others to eat them.

Now, if nowhere do we find this saying in the New Testament: * Do not eat this, it is evident that the distinctions of foods, which according to the laws were established, he made them cease, by the very fact that with sinners, and with tax collectors, and with Pharisees he ate and drank. And, (regarding) the

Passover, he said to his disciples: I ardently desired to eat this Passover with you. Will they say about the Passover that it was fish, not lamb? for Christ ate all kinds of food indiscriminately, as is evident in the Gospel.

Now, if they say that Christ, after his resurrection, ate fish, and not flesh, therefore we also eat fish, and not flesh; it must be said that: they must not now eat fish, but (only) during the resurrection, as Christ, after his resurrection, ate fish which he found among fishermen.

But the fish is flesh, this is obvious to all; for (every being) which has body and blood, fat and bone, it must be fleshy and living; and there is a fish on whose ribs, as on the ribs of a pig, there is a thick layer of fat, and blood gushes from it as much as from a sheep. And this fish eats filthy food that even wild animals and brutes do not eat; and this fish, we must rather call it a ferocious beast, it which eats its fellows indiscriminately; and, as much purer than him (fish) are the brutes, (some) of them in sacrifices and burnt offerings are offered to God, and among the fish, none.

But, in this symbol and example of the great mystery which was to be revealed, animals, small and large livestock, appeared, and not fish. As the lamb by whose blood the eldest sons of Israel were redeemed in Egypt, and the ram which was slain in place of Isaac, were the (figurative) thought of the true Lamb who takes away sins of the world; and also the heifer which outside the camp was immolated as a burnt offering: following the example of these animals, Christ also, outside the city, was tortured. And David said: Let it be acceptable to the Lord, like a tender (and delicate) veal, and not like a delicious fish; for the fish, although it comes as an apologue, comes as an apologue (figurative) of the tomb, not of vitality: according to what the Lord says that: As Jonah was in the belly of a fish three days and three nights, in the same way the Son of Man must enter into the heart of the earth and be there three days and three nights; and so we do not find in the holy books that (the Lord) sanctified the fish, and gave (it) as food, and commanded to abstain from meat as from impure and filthy food.

But even in the laws it is written that: I have given you brutes and birds to eat as well as vegetables and herbs; but only the dead animal (of itself) and the blood, do not eat; because the breath of the brute is his blood. And the apostles, in the epistle which they wrote from Jerusalem to Antioch, confirmed this (precept) to keep you from blood and from every animal that has been strangled, and from animals that have died (of themselves), and from fornication; and they said not of flesh. Moreover, in these (same) laws, the edible brutes, (God) calls them pure, and (those) not edible, impure; not that these brutes were impure by nature, but those not acceptable to the judgment of men, God calls them impure; for he knew that there is a certain animal that we enjoy eating, and a certain animal that we do not like to eat; and according to this he instituted his laws.

But nothing impure (comes) from food: from the Lord himself let us hear this: There is nothing that enters the belly of man that can defile man; but whatever comes out of man, that defiles man. And the apostle, having in advance by (effect of) prophecy the unjust pride of the sectaries, says: They cut off food, they prohibit the marriage that God has made for the consolation of the faithful, who with gratitude in enjoy; for (it is a thing) sanctified by the word of God and by prayers. Not that there is anything impure, and then sanctified; but that which to them appeared unclean because of the immolation, (concerning) this, the apostle says: it is sanctified by the word of God and by prayers. For this, in another epistle, he says that: * when one of the infidels invites you, and you go, of whatever is put before you, eat, and do not be scrupulous. From which it is evident that among all (this) was (included) the flesh. And then he says that: Of everything that is sold in the *macellum*, that is to say in the meat market, eat, and do not be scrupulous.

But they say that the Apostle says that: It is better not to eat flesh, nor to drink wine, that my brother may not thereby be offended; and then that: I will not eat meat forever, by which my brother would be scandalized.

We will say: If the brother is also scandalized by the fish, then we should not eat it.

For, because of the scandal, one should not eat, and no, because some impurity would be (coming from) food, and especially for wine by (the influence of) which many even stumble. Meat does not cause sin as much as wine, (which) depraves the drinkers, and scandalizes the spectators. And how is it (possible) that they keep themselves from the flesh, and not keep themselves from wine, these Marcionites? for this word (of the apostle), on both (substances, flesh and wine), rests: He says not to eat flesh, nor to drink wine; and of this (precept) producing the reasons, he says: (in order) that thereby my brother may not be scandalized or weaken. By this, it is demonstrated that because of the scandal, (the apostle) expressed this thought, and not because he considered these foods impure, he who says that: He is the one who believes (can) eat of all. * If you believe, he said, that by the word of God and prayers food is sanctified, eat, and do not discriminate. But, if you are weak in faith, and you have scruples, eat only plants, and do not be scandalized, and, when you do not believe (can) eat everything, as (food) pure, do not judge not the one who eats it: as also the one who eats it must not blame you, as a weak (man) who does not believe (to be able) to eat everything, as (food) pure; for it is not that food puts us before God, or withdraws us from his face, but it is either faith, or the scruple of the spirits and scandal.

13. Now, your religious people, they say, why are they deprived of flesh? Our religious people abstain from (certain) foods, not because they consider these foods impure, and products of matter as an impure thing. If, to consider these foods as impure, they had made a vow, their vow would count for nothing. But they abstain from these foods, so that the holiness which they have resolved to keep, they may keep more easily.

For this also, our fathers the holy bishops established canons; (ruling): If some believer does not eat meat, and vegetables are cooked with the meat, and if he does not want to eat these vegetables, let him be excommunicated: why? firstly because of the foods given by God he cannot regard them (as) abject; and then, so that he does not harm himself through unjust pride, as if thereby he were more than (other) men.

Moreover, the virgins of the holy Church keep their virginity, not because of this that they consider marriage, given by God, (as) defilement, as (do) Marcion, Mani, and the harlots; because, if in this spirit they made vows, their virginity would not be an honest virginity; but, to love God better, they renounce the good creatures of God, so that, resembling the angels of God, in whom there is neither male nor female, they show on earth the same virtue; according to what (is said) that there are eunuchs who became eunuchs for the kingdom of heaven, (in order) to be, at the resurrection, like the angels; and the apostle calls virgins faithful man. But, having regard to nature, he cannot give a formal order; but with a glance (preferably) he disposes, as the Lord also does, but he does not press.

14. All this for the sect of the Marcionites has been said, (for) them who reject marriage, and the use of meat: and, dedicated with the laity to virginity, they distort their vow; because, in order not to (be able to) resist concupiscence, they throw them once again into penitence.

But if they do not believe in the laws (of him) who says: A man will leave his father and his mother, and will go after his wife, and they will be two in one body; why should they not believe in Jesus, who confirms this (commandment), and adds: What God has joined together, let not man separate! Now, for the faithful who want to demonstrate the truth, first of all their business is this; as things are, so let them confess them. Then, if they become (men) elite in virtue, this is admissible. And not (let them do) like those people who annihilate what is greatest, (under the pretext) that from the pool (of baptism) we take a vow to abstain from the flesh, and from marriage; and then break their vow, and go to enter into penitence.

And, if you ask if torments exist (on the part of) the good being, they say: there do not exist. And if there is no fear of torments, is it not evident that they fear nothing of torments, and that they are indifferent in sin? But from him from whom there is no torment (to fear), there are no gifts (to hope for).

REFUTATIONS

But we, they say, have therefore fled from the righteous; for, fearful threats he threatens in his laws, (saying) that: The fire is kindled in my anger, and will consume (all) even in the inner depths; and all this was kept in my treasury. And elsewhere: God judges by fire.

O foolish and misguided (men)! if, because of terrible threats, you flee from the god of laws, when Jesus, with even more terrible threats, (threatens) the inextinguishable fire, the immortal worm, and eternal torments, where will you have to flee? And when in the Old and New Testaments we find the same threats and the same promises of goods, is it not evidently demonstrated that one giver is (donor) of the old and the new?

15. But, not believing in the resurrection of the body, whence (came this thought) to Marcion, to Mani, and other such people?

They say: the apostle said that: * The body and blood do not inherit the kingdom of God, and corruption (does not inherit) incorruptibility.

Then, that: I desired (ardently) to leave the body, and to be with the Lord; by which it is evident, they say, that since the body is made of matter, it is therefore not made worthy of resurrection.

And that, because the body is made of matter, it will not be made worthy of the kingdom, then, because from the just are (emanated) the (souls), (it is) not necessary that they be worthy of the kingdom of (being) good. But he refutes them, this same apostle, here in the same passage. Pointing as if with a finger at the body, he said that: Our corruption must take on incorruptibility, and this mortal (body) must take on immortality; from which it is evident that (it is) not souls that he calls corruptible and mortal, but bodies. And in another epistle he says that: It is (reserved) for us all to appear before the throne of Christ, that each one may receive with his body, (according) to what he has done before, either (in) good and be (in) bad. Do you see that with the body he says he carries good or evil, and not only with the soul.

REFUTATIONS

But they say: the apostle said that corruption does not inherit incorruptibility.

O collector of passages, O Marcion! he listens to one thing, and rejects the other. If, with a right mind, he would hear this, (knowing) that corruption does not inherit incorruptibility, he could stand (on the bounds of) the truth, for the apostle so confirms the resurrection of the body, that he even provides several examples.

First, the first (example) is Christ's own resurrection, (saying that): Christ died according to the Scriptures, and was buried, and rose again the third day. And, well established (on this subject), he shows several circumstances for the establishment of this resurrection; and moreover, this is what he cries in the ear of Marcion and Mani, and he says: If the dead do not rise, what will those who have been baptized for the dead do? You, says (Marcion), you say that bodies, because of matter they are (formed), do not resuscitate; if mortal bodies do not resurrect, souls, (them) alive, for dead bodies, why do they make a profession (of faith)? Or mortal bodies with living souls, why will they be baptized, if, as you say, mortal bodies should not be resurrected?

So we must understand this saying, and not like Marcion, (who) exaggerates (saying) that: Instead of a dead child, we must baptize his living neighbor, so that (the baptism) of his dead child may be counted; what, in fact, the Marcionites do; but it condemns them, this word of the Lord, (which says that): * Unless anyone is born again, he cannot see the kingdom of God. And then: * If anyone is not born of water and the spirit, he will not enter the kingdom of heaven. By which it is obvious that each individual must be baptized, and not one for the other.

And then, according to the apologue of the seeds, obviously demonstrated is the resurrection of the body. * As the seed you sowed, (so is the fruit). One does not come for another, although it takes on a thousand charming aspects. But you never sowed barley or reaped wheat; and you never sowed millet and reaped rye; but (to) what you have sown, you have reaped the same.

REFUTATIONS

According to this example, says (the apostle), also the body which has fallen, the same must rise again.

Then again, this saying of the apostle that: The body and blood do not inherit the kingdom of God, and that corruption does not inherit incorruptibility, must not be understood in the sense in which Marcion takes it, (know) that: because bodies are made of matter, they do not resuscitate; but in two other ways.

One in this (sense) that: when in the thoughts of the body and in its works is still man, animated are also the body and the blood; and, as according to the body only (man) thinks and acts, he is not worthy to enter the kingdom of heaven; as also in another epistle, the apostle writes to his disciples that: Those who are in the body think the thoughts of the body; but you are not in body, but in spirit. Was it that when he wrote this to his disciples, half were in the body, and half were not? From which it is evident that in body they were all, but not all in the works of the body, and (nor all in the works) of the spirit.

Then, in another sense, it must be understood that: not swollen with flesh and blood resurrect the bodies, but renewed by the resurrection; (from) corruptible as they were, they inherit incorruptibility; as also (the apostle) advances it by these (words, saying) that: The trumpet sounds, and the dead, who (are dead) in Christ, rise incorruptible, and we are renewed.

By this it is demonstrated that bodies renewed by resurrection, freed from all needs, rise again; and death is swallowed up in defeat, when (those bodies) corrupt put on incorruptibility, mortals (put on) immortality, sown by weakness (put on) strength, cast in contempt (put on) glory. And there is no body that will remain in the earth. But the soul of each, putting on the body of each, in the twinkling of an eye, (all) will stand before the terrible tribunal, some for eternal life, and others for the punishments of judgment.

16. This Marcion came from the country of Pontus, son of a bishop; and, having corrupted a virgin, he fled, because his father himself had separated him

from the Church, and having gone to Rome to seek penance at that time, and not having achieved it, he lost his temper against the faith. And, putting forward three (propositions), he teaches (and deals with) good, just, and evil; and, the New Testament, he considers different from the old, and, according to what was said in it, he despises (and rejects) the resurrection of the body. And baptism he gives not only one, but three after having sinned; and, in place of dead children, he urges others to receive the seal (of baptism). And he is so impudent that he orders women to give baptism, which no one has been able to do in other sects, nor to give baptism two or three times, nor to take women as priests.

Moreover, from where did the priesthood come to him, (to him) who, having corrupted a virgin, was removed from the Church by his father, when he was not even worthy of attaining penance? And indeed, he was not worthy of it, because, on the orders of the Holy Spirit, he dared to throw out his hand, to cut off, to reject a part as (thing) useless, and to choose, and to take the other (part). as useful. And he does not know that: when you cut a finger from the body, this small cut part affects all (the parts) of the body. Even more, (Marcion) is condemned by (Jesus Christ) coming to perfect the laws, who said: I have not come to dissolve the laws and the prophets, but to fulfill them. And by the apostle, who says that: Christ is our peace, he who made both in one: Glory to him in the eternity of eternity! *Amen* .

ADVICE FROM THE SAME DOCTOR EZNIK GORHPATZI

1. He who loves God, guards himself from his own will as from an enemy.

2. It is better with pure thoughts to sleep, than with impure thoughts to offer prayers (to God), and not receive wages, and to labor in vain.

3. Mortify your body with rigor (of penance), and your heart with the fear of God, so that you are without fear of the deadly arrows of Satan.

4. He who loves the fear (of God) raises up a statue of love to God, and irreconcilable enmity to Satan.

5. Love and fear (of God) make it for you a (second nature, so) that for illusion you do not work.

6. As much as you will experience privations, fatigue, sorrows, if you endure (all this, so much) you will prepare for yourself incorruptible treasures in the heavens; but, if you murmur, and (if you) have a heavy heart, in vain you work, and without remuneration you remain.

7. Strengthen yourself by the thought of Christ's passion, and bear (all) for him, so that you may enjoy his immutable benefits.

8. He who rests in spring, but in winter is overwhelmed by hunger and freezing cold.

9. He who here (low) fattens his body, enters into eternal rest.

10. Obey with love, pray with hope, work with faith, and you will be glorified at the heavenly wedding.

11. Use whatever grace God gives you for the needs of the unfortunate, so that grace may flow (upon you) and you may be glorified.

12. The sensual religious person is like a swine; in a sea of sins he immerses himself.

13. Tears are (like) water that washes away sins, and sighs (like) penance. So whoever spends all his time in (observing) religious rules, in mourning and in sadness, what blessed glory will he inherit?

14. A religious hypocrite is (like) the (deceptive) veil of Satan; having Satan all around him, he hides the ugliness of his members, and, by an illuminated veil, he deceives the spectators. These people are wolves covered in lambskins whom Christ threatened to classify among the unbelievers.

15. He who sees his brother, and remains sad, is overcome by hypocrisy; he who sits alone, (on his side), and is cheerful, is a prisoner of Satan.

16. Our mouths are (infected with the) odor of fasting, and our tongues numbed by the singing of psalms; and, what God asks, we do not have, love and humility; with our lips we love God, and in vain we labor.

17. They do not eat the flesh of the brute, and they eat their brothers insatiably; they drink no wine, and they defile their souls with blood; they hate married (people), and, through their impure thinking, they continually fornicate; they put on scant clothing, and by avarice they are consumed. From such people it is necessary to distance oneself, and not to have (with them) communication.

REFUTATIONS

18. A monk should not live together with young boys; for the shooting of arrows, which comes from them, is worse than the venom of vipers.

19. A cheerful religious man is the *Gergesean demon.

20. A young religious who is not at the feet of old men is the easy prey of Satan.

21. To a younger religious (than you) do not tell your secrets, because it is his death.

22. The glare of the eyes, the smoke offends it; and the glory of the religious, the association with young boys (the offusque). If he opens the heavens, do not enter; if he has angelic morals, don't believe him.

23. Do not love food and drink to the full, otherwise you will build your body (into) a city of fornication, and (into) a fortress of Satan.

24. Wine awakens a host of evils and drives away the fear of God.

25. Do not love your brother, (by killing him) with food, delicate drinks, magnificent clothes, so that you do not inherit the punishment of Cain.

26. Do not grieve anyone, nor be saddened by anyone.

27. Do not be angry with a disciple who has failed; for a sick person is not, by his will, sick.

28. The love of God is (like) the particular reproach (of our faults).

REFUTATIONS

29. Do not inject the poison (of anger) against a brother, under the pretext of admonition.

30. A delicate remedy heals the wound, and kindness (cures) the ills.

31. Labor with satisfaction (and gratitude) without crown (or without reward) does not remain.

32. The luxurious religious person is (like) the habitation of the devil.

33. He who covets bodily goods commits fornication.

34. If you are persecuted for God's sake, do not hold a grudge.

35. When you pray, choose your thoughts, and then chant.

36. If you do not pray for your enemy as for yourself, it is better not to pray.

37. If you receive something from someone, add it to your usual prayers.

38. The demons concentrate in goods, and the angels (delight) in distributing them.

39. The love of goods is (as it were) attached to the yoke of idolatry.

40. Prayers (emanating) from a holy heart bring salvation from sacrifice.

41. Don't look for the flavor of food.

REFUTATIONS

42. He sees Christ, who hates (earthly) goods.

43. For a religious person, a fortified place means tranquility.

44. A religious man, friend of his brothers, is related to Christ.

45. A peaceful religious person is the shining torch of fraternity.

46. He who has a grudge against his brother is bound by a pact with Satan. He who falls asleep with hatred irritates God.

47. In the evening, when you climb into bed, think that you have descended into the tomb.

48. Leave behind thoughts and futile and vain things, and hold fast to the fear of God, and meditate on the day of judgment.

49. He who deprives his brother of bodily food does not desire the table of Christ.

50. He who hastens to take something from someone has no hope in Christ.

51. If anyone asks anything from you, and (you) give it to him, thank God, for you have gained more than that.

52. Do not be jovial and buffoonish, so that you do not inherit endless tears.

53. With humility and hope to obey, and with knowledge to work, this is (there) perfection.

54. Others are the virtues, and others are the (vessels of) election.

55. He commanded you to eat the bread of the day in the sweat of (your brow), and you want to inherit eternal life in sleep. Seventy years are assigned to your life, even in pain and affliction. You want to have a thousand years of pain-free life.

56. To the weary he commanded rest, and not to the sensual men, fattened fodder for worms.

57. Repress your gloomy character by abstinence, soften the hardness of your heart by (continual) vigilance, dry up the damp (impurity) of your body by work, and then you can bear the cross of Christ. Teach your heart to love its brother. And so, love your body, like an insidious brother.

58. To hate the fear (of God), to love without fearing anything, is one and the same evil.

59. If with compassion you do not love your brother, you can do nothing with him.

60. Mortify your body by (your application to) the knowledge of the (holy) books, and the observance of their testimony.

61. There are virtues which are not pleasing to God: they are the deception of evil.

62. Delicacy and rest, hai (all this).

63. What (each) of the brothers needs, give it to him.

64. Tomorrow you must go to your homeland, there, rest.

65. When you pray, know well with whom you are speaking, or what you are asking. (Your) thoughts within you, collect them.

66. When God sends you delicious food, or pure bread (wheat), Christ's portion to an unfortunate brother, give it before your meal, so that Christ may be your companion.

67. When you sit down at the table, lower your head; see nothing but yourself alone, and eat gratefully.

68. Do not seek sweetness in food or satiety, but only that which (from hunger) removes danger.

69. Let your clothes not be (made) to adorn your person, but only for the needs of your body; but, if you love the superfluous, the dishonest, you are deprived of celestial ornaments.

70. If you are sick or tired, do not behave with authority.

71. If you are given friendship, thank God, and if you are not (friended), do not be saddened, and do not sadden anyone; but mortify yourself a little by the silence; because he who fights needs resignation.

72. Meditate (within yourself) on the day of judgment which God has prepared.

73. This life is a struggle.

REFUTATIONS

74. He who is good appears cheerful.

75. Let us seek what Christ has promised to give, (saying) that: * Where I am, there also my servants will be.

76. Old age and illness are a temporary struggle; because the strength of the body is failing, the danger multiplied, the rest little (lasting) or (there is) none at all: and Satan inflames the furnace of his anger, and makes order hated, blasphemy of the superior, murmur against the brothers; here there is need of love and pity, of long-suffering, and of taking the crown of martyrdom.

77. He who is angry with his brother, and is not for God, the merciless angel stands before him.

78. He who, while chanting, laughs, or intersperses worldly words, let him be (put) apart from holy things, until he becomes well!

79. It is better to lift up one's hands to God when one prays, but more precious (in work) is he who, in the needs of his brothers, will serve.

80. If you trust in your brother, obey him; but otherwise, the custom does not come out.

81. A religious person must, even at the price of his blood, resist carnal desires, and thus, make a (living) sacrifice to God.

82. Christ said: * I am the way, and the truth, and the life; and whoever wants to come to me, let him deny himself, and take up the cross, and come after me. And he who does not deny himself cannot bear the cross of Christ, and is not a partaker of the truth. And he who is not (a partaker) of the truth cannot possess life in eternity, but in shadow he stands and in darkness he wanders.

REFUTATIONS

83. And he who cultivates his own wills cannot accomplish worldly work, even less spiritual work, although he spends his life in great fatigue, he cannot achieve religious rule. Obedient, although soft and cowardly, he is religious, (it is true, but) he is in bondage in the house of God.

84. The idle bee is better than the working wasp.

85. He who has renounced himself, and under the yoke of command has entered, carrying the cross of Christ, must not choose the orders of the superior, but (well) obey with fear; for even Peter was girded by the commandment; and, if you are at fault towards the superior, nothing is possible with him, because you lose your soul. Sometimes you complain, sometimes you blaspheme, sometimes you fight, sometimes near others you backbite; love and obedience you take away (from the hearts) of the brothers, you teach impiety to all. Of such a (man), the alliance is already (title of) condemnation.

86. Without knowing, without discernment, a superior, by (wanting) to heal, wounds, and, by wanting to rectify, breaks. Instead of love, it shows hatred, and instead of hatred, love. And, by disturbing (thus) the brothers, he leaves them without merit (any).

87. He who is the (main) column and in it constitutes the whole building, if it is overturned, (drags and) puts everything down; in the same way the superior, if, according to the will of God, he does not lead the entire meeting of the brothers, he hands it over to Satan, and, instead of (wise) direction, of perdition he becomes the cause. Great heartbreak, incurable evils is such a direction; for men look more to example than to truth.

88. He who scandalizes one (only) of the little ones is not worthy of the grave; Now, what do you say about him who is the cause of destruction for many? Was he not a cooperator with Satan, and with him must be tormented in hell.

89. The spiritual superior is a divine fire, it burns, (consumes) the corrupting evil, dries up the (impure) humidity of the hearts, and by religious rule tests like gold in the furnace, and in a (state of) sanctification, undefiled offers the brothers to God, and he himself (higher) * according to the faithful servant, reigns over ten cities.

90. An avaricious superior, who is (the same thing as) an idolater, is a leader of bandits; there are many bandits in the world, and they are not all murderers; but he (avaricious superior) commits murder every day. Not only does he murder the body, as a thief would do, but he becomes a cooperator with Satan, and loses the soul entrusted to him. He easily carries out all evil, and never good.

91. If the illness of all (and each of the) brothers does not distress you, do not be superior.

92. If what is unworthy, according to need, you do not rebuke, do not be a doctor.

93. Honey is sweet, but it harms the body of the sick; useful is advice and reproof, but for one who has his face (turned) toward the west, it is useless.

(Here) the precepts are finished.

REFUTATIONS

The Scriptorium Project is the work of a small group of lay people of various apostolic churches who are interested in the preservation, transmission, and translation of the works of the early and medieval church. Our efforts are to make the works of the church fathers accessible to anyone who might have an interest in Christian antiquities and the theological, philosophical, and moral writings that have become the bedrock of Western Civilization.

To-date, our releases have pulled from the Greek, Syriac, Georgian, Latin, Celtic, Ethiopian, and Coptic traditions of Christianity, and have been pulled from sundry local traditions and languages.

REFUTATIONS

Other Selections from the Armenian Church Series:

Refutations by Eznik of Kolb (Dec. 2007)

Explanation of the Faith of the Armenian Church by Nerses IV the Gracious, Catholicos of Armenia (July 2009)

The Life of Mashtots by Koriun the Iberian (Nov. 2012)

Letter to Kiwron, Catholicos of Iberia by Movses II, Catholic of Armenia (Nov. 2013)

Canons of the Synod of Partav by Sion I, Catholicos of Armenia (Dec. 2013)

The History of the Holy Cross of Aparank by St. Gregory of Narek (Feb. 2014)

Armenian Synaxarium: Volume I- Month of Navasard (Oct. 2018)

The Geography by Ananias of Shirak (Dec. 2020)

REFUTATIONS

www.ingramcontent.com/pod-product-compliance
Lightning Source LLC
LaVergne TN
LVHW021829060526
838201LV00058B/3568